CÉSAR FRANCK

Franck at the organ

NORMAN DEMUTH

César Franck

London

DENNIS DOBSON LTD

First published in Great Britain in MCMXLIX by
DENNIS DOBSON LTD, 12 Park Place, St. James's,
London SW1.   All rights reserved.   Made and
printed in Great Britain by RICHMOND HILL
PRINTING WORKS LTD, Bournemouth.

109/R

Contents

Foreword   7

Chapter One   1822-1837   11

        Two   1838-1871   18

        Three   1872-1890-1922   33

        Four   General Characteristics of his Music   44

        Five   The Orchestral Works   61

        Six   The Organ Works   95

        Seven   The Chamber Works   123

        Eight   The Piano Works   143

        Nine   The Choral Works   156

        Ten   The Operas   172

        Eleven   The Songs and Church Music   178

        Twelve   The Franck Family   186

        Thirteen   Franck's Contemporaries   198

        Fourteen   The Man—Summary   205

Appendix A   List of books consulted   215

          B   List of works   216

List of Illustrations

FACING
PAGE

Franck at the organ   3
   (From the painting by J. Rongier)

César Franck in 1845   60
   (Mme Chopy-César Franck)

'Ce qu'on entend sur la montagne'   61
   (Bibliothèque National)

First page of the subscription list for 'Trois Trios   102
   Concertantes'
   (Bibliothèque National)

Pastorale   103
   (Bibliothèque National)

César Franck in 1870   160
   (Pierre Petite)

Guy Ropartz, Pierre de Bréville, Vincent d'Indy   161
   (Lipnitski, Rouart-Lerolle, Henri Manuel)

César Franck in 1889   194
   (Mme Chopy-César Franck)

Schola Cantorum   195
   (Yvon)

6

Foreword

In order to avoid the exasperation of constantly referring to footnotes, to find that they merely quote the authority for some statement, I have placed all the sources of information and other books consulted in one list in Appendix 'A'. Since facts cannot be gainsaid, there is no reason to acknowledge their source, but where opinion or theory are concerned, the acknowledgement will be found in the text.

In this, the first book by an English author on César Franck, the reader will find a certain amount of repetition. The book is intended for reference purposes as well as for general reading and there are several instances of statements appearing in the biographical section which must reappear in the consideration of the works. There are not so many that the general reader will experience any annoyance, but if books of this nature are planned solely for reading from cover to cover, they lose half their value. In every case save one, all works are referred to in their original language.

I would like to express my gratitude to MM Pierre de Bréville and J. Guy Ropartz, the only surviving direct pupils of Franck, for all their trouble in putting me right on many matters over which a false impression has been created. Without their help the book would have been inaccurate and lacking in some of its most interesting features.

I would thank the authorities of the Bibliothèque Nationale and the Paris Conservatoire for placing at my disposal the many Franck MSS in their possession and for giving me all

7

facilities for study, as well as a hearty welcome; Mlle A. Dieu-donné for lending me the typescript of her 'communication' to the Société Française de Musicologie; M Guy de Lioncourt, Director of the École César Franck, for giving me all information as to the Schola Cantorum and subsequent events; the Lord Chamberlain's Office for allowing me to search (in vain) for records of Franck's visit to Queen Victoria's Library; the Registrar General and Mr E. H. Searle, Registrar of Greenwich, for digging up the certificate of the wedding of Franck's son (I hope that the Franck consciousness which this research aroused will long continue!); my friends Godfrey Sampson and J. A. Sowerbutts for lending me music otherwise unobtainable, and, in the latter case, for reading through the first draft; my pupil Ronald Meachen who read the proofs, and, lastly, my wife, who made an excellent secretary in Paris and saved me considerable labour.

The following publishers have kindly allowed me to use extracts from the works in their possession and their co-operation is gratefully acknowledged.

MM Durand et Cie
    Six Pièces pour grand orgue
    Trois Pièces pour grand orgue
    Trois Chorals

MM Enoch et Cie
    Prélude, Choral, et Fugue
    Les Eolides
    Variations symphoniques
    'La Vase brisé'
    'Nocturne'

MM Hamelle et Cie
    Quintet
    Quartet
    Symphony
    Violin Sonata
    Prélude, Aria, et Final

MM Heugel et Cie
    Rédemption
    Ruth

MM Bornemann et Cie
   Psyché

MM Joubert et Cie
   Les Béatitudes

MM Lemoine et Cie
   Le Chasseur maudit

I have been unable to trace the present owners of 'Paris', but if this should attract their notice perhaps they would accept my apologies and assurance that it will be put right in subsequent editions.

Photographic reproductions are acknowledged in each separate case and my best thanks are due to all those who arranged for these to be done. I must however express my thanks separately to Mme Chopy-César-Franck for sending the two hitherto unpublished photographs of her grandfather.

1822-1837

To place a composer of whatever importance in his right perspective, it is necessary to take stock of the situation of music in Europe at the time of his birth. Those composers who on their death have left a definite imprint on the face of music, and whose influence was at that time already being felt, often afford an interesting contrast to their surroundings and contemporaries. It is not always realized how closely interlocked were the lives of the great hierarchy of all nations and how the pendulum swung from one culture to another. It is not essential, however, for a composer to have been great in his music for him to be the link between generations. Such a one was Camille Saint-Saëns whose longevity witnessed the phenomenal progress of French music from Berlioz, through Franck, Debussy and Ravel, to the ebullient days of 'Les Six'. His life also witnessed the gradual decline of the Teutonic tradition from supremacy to insignificance, he himself succumbing in turn to the prevailing influences which one by one he cast aside, never, however, finding any peculiar individuality.

One regards Haydn, for example, as being almost antedeluvian until the realization dawns that Berlioz's *Symphonie fantastique* was composed only twenty-one years after Haydn's death, and that Berlioz himself was, in fact, alive when Haydn died. Coming to living memory, Sibelius was born four years before the death of Berlioz.

The prophet, however, becomes important only in retrospect, and the thrill which is experienced when we realize that the person we are talking to is an intimate friend of, say, Sibelius is not as great as that experienced if that person had been a friend of Elgar or Ravel. The panorama of musical history when spread out before our eyes brings the subject into relief and from it we can make our assessment.

César Auguste Franck was born at Rue Neuve Saint Pierre, Maison Thomson (Sans nr.), Paroisse, St. Croix, in Liége on 22nd December 1822. Liége had been the birthplace of an earlier composer who became enfolded in the tradition of French music, Grétry, who was born in 1741, dying in Paris in 1831. Of the representative musicians of the period, their names give the clue to the whole situation in Paris. Cherubini was sixty-two and his career as Director of the Conservatoire was finishing. His music was gradually failing in power and he himself was disillusioned and embittered. His operas were performed from time to time, arousing the irascibility of Berlioz, then in the full flood of rebellion. Spontini was fifty-four. This martinet of the opera, a unique figure, had already composed his greatest works, *La Vestale* and *Fernand Cortez; Olympie* had been written and produced in Paris in 1819, to be revived in Berlin in 1821. Boïeldieu, more an historical than a creative figure, was forty-three and had not yet written his masterpiece *La Dame Blanche*. Auber, the only survivor musically today, was forty. He was experiencing a series of failures and had not yet composed *Masaniello*, *Fra Diavolo* or *Le Cheval de bronze*. Of the younger ones, Meyerbeer was thirty-one and had not yet written either *Robert le Diable* or *Les Huguenots*. Rossini, a year younger, had already composed *Le Barbier de Séville*. Of the rising generation, Berlioz was nineteen, Gounod four, and Offenbach three.

All these names were primarily connected with opera. Symphonic music in Paris was practically at a standstill, creatively speaking, and had been so since the days of Gossec.

Other than Berlioz, the composers in their 'teens were Glinka (nineteen) and Mendelssohn (thirteen). Schumann and Chopin were twelve and Liszt eleven.

In this country things were even worse. The highlight was Dr William Crotch, the first Principal of the Royal Academy of Music and the composer of the first British Symphony, of which only a flute part seems to have survived. Crotch was followed by Cipriani Potter, a pupil of Beethoven and the first British composer to develop along symphonic lines of any proportion. The only other name was Bishop, then twenty-six years old, an indefatigable composer of moribund operas for Covent Garden and later to become Sir Henry Rowley Bishop.

How many of these composers have survived to any large degree other than as historical figures? Auber is remembered by some of the overtures to the operas, Rossini likewise, with the addition of *Le Barbier* and some arias. Meyerbeer proved a dead horse when an attempt was made to revive *Les Huguenots* in London some years ago. Only in Germany was there any promise on a large or important scale and there romantic music had become formulated. Weber was thirty-six and had composed both *Der Freischütz* and the *Concertstück* for piano and orchestra. *Euryanthe* followed in 1823—and Weber's operas *in toto* are impossible nowadays.

However the year 1822 was important for one great achievement. Beethoven finished his Op. 111 (the last piano sonata) and received an invitation from the Philharmonic Society of London, offering him fifty pounds for a new symphony. He had already commenced his ninth and completed it in 1823. The Philharmonic, therefore, got rather more than it bargained for. He actually put the finishing touches to the Mass in D on the birthday of Franck. Vincent d'Indy sees in this coincidence some kind of divine continuity.

The Franck family traced its descent through a line of Walloon painters, the earliest of whom was Jérome Franck, born in 1549 and dying in Paris in 1610, thus establishing the precedent for Franck emigration. Franck's father was a hard-headed business man in the banking profession. A contemporary photo of him shows a hard, stern and forbidding countenance which would brook no nonsense from anybody, least of all his own family. Cortot describes him as a 'little bank clerk'. In any case, whatever the position was, he numbered several well-known artists of all kinds among his friends and covered the prosaic routine of his business life with an artistic veneer. His other son, Joseph, was also musically inclined and it was decided that both boys should 'go in for music', César, at any rate, having shown uncommon signs of ability in this direction.

César was sent to the Liége Conservatoire. This institution was founded in 1827 and was originally called 'L'Ecole royale de Musique'. The state took it over in 1832 and renamed it. The Director, when Franck entered, was Daussoigne, a nephew of the French composer Méhul. Daussoigne basked in this reflected glory by hyphenating his own name with that of his distinguished uncle. Franck was extremely fortunate in his teachers. Daussoigne taught harmony through progressive counterpoint, in contradistinction to the system at the Paris Conservatoire where the two subjects were treated as separate studies. Franck was an exceptional boy in every way. In 1832, at the age of nine and a half, he won the first prize for solfège.

This prize consisted of an enormous bound volume of piano compositions by Hummel. The winner evidently felt that he ought to study the whole book and the youthful fingering marks written in pencil testify to his zeal.

In 1834, at the age of eleven, he won the first prize for piano, the reward being a full score of *Robert le Diable*. This pleased his father immensely because the career he had planned for his son was that of a virtuoso pianist. However, in the more congenial and important realms of harmony and counterpoint, Franck made astonishing strides and it would appear from the dates on his books of exercises that he finished the study of harmony on 29th January 1836, no mean accomplishment for a schoolboy. Nevertheless, we may note here that this stood him in no good stead afterwards, because he had to go through the whole course again at the Paris Conservatoire.

The three bound volumes of exercises are written in the neatest copperplate writing, an unusual thing for a boy of eleven; but these are nothing compared with a book of arithmetic problems, mainly dealing with foreign currencies which he worked at at the age of seven.

During this period the first works were composed and these are by no means merely boyish effusions, for they show a grasp of piano technique and musical construction extraordinarily mature for one of his age. The MSS in existence begin with Op. 5, *Variations Brillantes sur l'air du Pré aux Clercs* for piano were written in June 1834. A *Grand Trio* followed, succeeded by some more *Variations Brillantes*, this time *sur la Ronde favorite de*

Gustave III. These appeared in two forms, for piano alone, and with orchestral accompaniment. The *Première Grande Sonate pour le Piano Forte* was composed in 1835 and is described as being by César Auguste Franck de Liége, this description being used in order to differentiate the composer from one Edouard Franck who lived in Berlin. It is an extremely useful description as it assists in determining the dates of the early unpublished works.

This first *Grande Sonate* is by no means negligible in quality and shows the earliest tendencies towards the cyclic form. After Op. 10, *Première Grande Fantaisie* for piano came *Première Symphonie à Grand Orchestre* in G major. A note on the cover says that it was 'Executé à la Société plar. d'Orléans, le 16 fevrier 1841'. It certainly is for full orchestra; the full orchestra plays nearly all the time. There is no mention of the exact date of composition but it is labelled Op. 13 and the performance was much later. The tireless young man proceeded by easy stages to his *Deuxième Sonate pour piano* Op. 18 and then produced a number of short piano pieces, including a *Ballade irlandaise* and a *Mélodie* and *Air écossais.*

Franck's father decided to put his son's gifts to immediate profit and arranged a concert tour from Liége to Gand, Louvain, Brussels, and Malines. The youthful prodigy did not suffer in any way from this premature exploitation; on the contrary, it stimulated him to work, and in 1835 the entire family moved to Paris. Franck was too young to enter the Conservatoire, so he became a private pupil of Antonin Reicha. Again luck was with him in his teacher, and we must pause to consider this great professor.

Antonin Reicha was a Bohemian, and was born at Prague in 1770. He was much travelled and in the early days of his career played in the Electoral Orchestra at Bonn where he had as companion a certain Ludwig van Beethoven. He eventually became Professor at the Paris Conservatoire through the good graces of Louis XVIII, to the disgust of Cherubini and Fétis. He proved himself a thorough progressive. Setting his face against all pedantry, although a firm believer in musical discipline, he soon got across authority by insisting that a fugue was a work of art and not a mere technical exercise. He wrote several treatises on harmony and counterpoint in which he extolled polymodality and polytonality, going so far as to state categorically that music would be considerably enriched if composers would write in quarter-tones, thereby obtaining a closer approach to ordinary declamation. He was the first to draw attention to the lack of familiarity with national airs, prevalent at the period. His harmony instruction was not confined to vocal writing and he carefully explained the differences between it and writing for wind and for strings. He was naïve to a degree and although he could have used examples from the great composers, he said he thought that it would be more interesting if he wrote his own. . . . For its period his treatise on dramatic composition is masterly. The student is taken through the various steps of operatic composition and is shown the process of composition of a whole act— of Reicha's own opera, *Natalie*, which after some difficulty had had a few performances at the Paris Opera.

His masterpiece in the field of treatise was his *Trente-six Fugues pour le Piano-forte composées d'après un nouveau-système.*

His compositions aptly illustrate his theories. He placed great importance on rhythm and encouraged the use of 5/2 and 5/4 time. Indeed, he wrote an Overture for orchestra in 5/8 time, a spirited little work which is more than a curiosity even today. He believed in no stereotyped orchestra and was an enthusiast for wind instruments. As a composer he had quite a reputation. In *Les Employés* Balzac makes one of his characters say 'You must come to our house and hear a concert next Tuesday; they are playing a quintet by Reicha.'

He was a philosopher, and quoted Aristotle and Kant to his pupils. This did not appeal to Berlioz, Liszt, or Gounod, but it did appeal to Franck, although circumstances prevented him from pursuing his own investigations for some time.

This brief outline will show why Reicha was so good for Franck and so bad for Cherubini and Fétis. Marmontel, a pupil of the pianist Zimmerman, mentions the oblique looks which passed in the hall of the Conservatoire between 'Italy (Cherubini), Bohemia (Reicha) and Holland (Fétis)'. Like professor, like student, and many years later the position was to be the same with Franck and his generation. There must be some kind of divine direction in these matters. What would have happened if Franck had been sent to Halévy, for example?

Reicha found his pupil congenial in every way and Franck eagerly absorbed those works of Bach and Handel which Reicha transcribed for the piano for his pupils, as well as the then unknown masterpieces of old French music which few bothered about at the time. Unfortunately Reicha died in 1836, a fact which Franck noted at the end of his exercise book on a strip of thin brown paper pasted along the bottom of the page.

Franck's book of exercises could well serve today as a model for those students who think that any old piece of paper will do. These books in themselves are a complete course in the subjects. Reicha corrected the pupil's errors very tidily and such is the clarity that the reader can get a complete insight into his methods. Although Berlioz preferred Leseur to Reicha as a professor, he admitted the extreme clearness of the latter's explanations. The manner in which Reicha adapted orchestral resources to the peculiar need of the circumstances largely influenced Berlioz, and an examination of Reicha's scores shows clearly how Berlioz got his ideas and proves him to have been entirely inventive in his statement that no one knew anything about orchestration at the Conservatoire. In parenthesis, exactly what did Berlioz hope to gain by his attitude towards the contemporary musicians there?

Adolphe Adam, a composer far outside the orbit of academic music, testifies to the fact that the counterpoint course with Reicha took but one year, whereas with the other professors it took five.

From this period dates the friendship between Franck and Liszt which was broken only by the death of the latter, a friendship which proved of immense benefit to both musicians.

Chapter Two

1838-1871

Rᴇɪᴄʜᴀ's class was taken over by Leborne and in 1837 Franck entered the Conservatoire, studying harmony and counterpoint with Reicha's successor, and piano with Zimmerman. Leborne (Aimé Ambrose Simon) was born in Brussels in 1797. He was a pupil of Cherubini at the Conservatoire, winning the Prix de Rome in 1820. He was librarian at the Opéra and the Chapel of Napoleon III. Although principally a teacher (he wrote a treatise on harmony which was never published) he was also a composer of 'opéras-comiques' which have left no impression. Later, Franck was to have a pupil of the same name, but there is no evidence to show that the two Leborne's were in any way related. Leborne, the professor, died in 1866.

Zimmerman was one of the most distinguished teachers of the day, his most famous pupil being Marmontel who succeeded him at the Conservatoire. He published a treatise on harmony and counterpoint, to be studied at the keyboard, an early instance of an approach which has become established in recent years—it is quite remarkable to read of these early principles (those of Reicha as well as Zimmerman) in the light of what has been written, talked about, and practised in the present century as completely 'new'.

The Conservatoire was presided over by Cherubini, a pedant at heart, a disciplinarian, and a follower of the letter of the law. In 1823 he had refused admission to Liszt on the grounds that Liszt was a foreigner. Apparently he must have waived the law or caused the position to be altered by the time Franck presented himself, for there is no account of any difficulty. Today

18

a student of any nationality can join and is granted full rights and privileges. The history of the Conservatoire is one of continuous rebellion. These rebels were not of the ilk which is content to grumble in silence. We have but to read Berlioz's autobiography to get a complete and cheerful picture of the state of things and although Berlioz usually coloured every experience which suggested hostility to himself, there is no reason to discount anything in this connection. Nevertheless, nearly all France's greatest musicians have emanated from there. Cherubini, however, has been much maligned. Although ranged against any kind of innovation on the part of the professors, he was not antagonistic to any student who showed promise, and at least tolerated him provided that he behaved himself (which Berlioz certainly did not). Franck was all for a little rebellion on his own account.

Counterpoint proved instinctive with him, and his exercise book demonstrates this. The course at the Conservatoire today would be considered pretty stiff by most of the students at our institutions. In those days it was also dull and unimaginative, but to the pupil who had been taught from the very first that every exercise he wrote was 'composition' and not merely an 'exercise', it was full of possibilities. Franck was not bound by any laws or customs, but he always justified himself. His workings of the various examination fugues admit that he broke some of the 'rules'. Neatly written over the offending passages we read 'If I have written hidden fifths . . . I have done so in order to have complete chords'—'This passage is a little risky, but I thought I might write it in order to maintain the chromatic character of the subject.' However, the prime instance of an indisputable authority appears when he points out that a certain licence is permitted, authority 'Traité de contrepont et fugue de Mr (sic) Cherubini, page 64.' This knowledge of the Director's work must have proved gratifying to the Director and flooring to the examiners.

At the end of the first year Franck was awarded a 'proxime accessit' for fugue. He then astounded and confounded the authorities by an unwarrantable display of enterprise which had no parallel in the annals of the institution. Having played Hummel's Piano Concerto in A minor with considerable élan, he came to the sight reading test, which for reasons best known to himself, he transposed down a third. This was entirely unpremeditated and he played it in the new key without a falter. The examiners were flabbergasted. There was no rule forbidding this irregularity except that of failure to carry it out satisfactorily but such freedom of action could not be tolerated, no matter how clever it might have been. However, since he had played the required test perfectly accurately, he could hardly be said to have failed. Cherubini, feeling that this was an exceptional case (especially with a boy of fifteen), relented sufficiently to award him a 'Grand Prix d'Honneur', which sounded infinitely more imposing than the normal award.

The examination in fugue in 1838 called for one in eight parts for double choir, with five invertible subjects, and this after a year's study. That year Franck won the first prize for piano, the full score of *Figaro*. During his student career he actually won eight prizes; those mentioned, a full score of *Don Juan*, a full score of Gluck's *Alceste*, and a magnificently bound and signed copy of the full score of Cherubini's Requiem Mass which Franck won in 1839 at the age of sixteen for counterpoint and fugue—and this was only for second place. The seventh prize, however, was the most valuable because it consisted of the 5th, 6th and 7th symphonies of Beethoven whose works had but recently penetrated into Paris's musical conscience. This was in 1840 and was the first prize for fugue, a triple one in four parts, the subjects being written by Cherubini. It was, and still is, the custom at the Conservatoire to return the exercises, this laudable practice being considered an impediment to any partiality on the part of the examiners and also sufficient justification for results in both directions. Franck's fugue is almost monumental. He had a passing regard for it, for he made several copies for distribution to his friends and even presented his fiancée with one dedicated to her. It is possible that he was rather a prig. His exercises were always signed in full 'César Auguste Franck de Liége' and on the MS of one of them someone wrote the word 'pompier'.

He studied organ with François Benoist and in 1841 tried for the organ prize. The tests were severe and consisted of the accompaniment to a selected plainchant, the performance of an organ piece, the improvisation of a fugue and of a movement in sonata form, the themes being handed to the candidates by the examiners. Franck noticed that the fugue subject would combine with that of the sonata movement and proceeded to put the combination into effect. His invention ran away with him and he could not or would not stop. This so incensed the examiners that they flatly refused to give him an award of any kind, but Benoist persuaded them to reconsider their decision, and eventually Franck was awarded second prize. This was a copy of Rossini's *Guillaume Tell*. Cherubini, incidentally, was absent through illness.

In 1842 and 1843 he composed his first serious works, his 'official' Op. 1—*Trois trios concertans* for violin, cello, and piano. The designation of Op. 1 thus precluded publication of any of the earlier works.

His father decided to have them published by subscription. The price was forty-five francs to non-subscribers but a mere twelve francs to those who signed along the dotted line. To hold in one's hand the subscription list is to hold the signatures of nearly all the representative musicians in Paris at the time. The list is headed by Meyerbeer, followed by Auber, Berton, Urban, Louis and Adolphe Adam, Donizetti, Halévy, Chopin, Pleyel, Onslow (considered by Berlioz the greatest living *French* composer) and Ambroise Thomas. The nobility and gentry who risked twelve francs in a good cause included Baron James de Rothschild, the then Belgian Ambassador, and Comtesse Rezia d'Indy. The last was the grandmother of Franck's famous pupil, Vincent d'Indy. Her son, Wilfrid d'Indy, was already one of his pupils and turned out to be an amateur composer of some ability. Among the ordinary folk was Josephine Desmousseaux, the future mother-in-law of the composer.

Looking at the names we are bound to agree that every encouragement was given to the young composer by those in high position. A pleasant theory, this. An unpleasant one is that they did not wish to be omitted from anything and felt that by subscribing twelve francs they were gaining some prestige. One would like to think the former, but the conditions of intrigue prevalent among the Paris musicians at the time forces us to believe that the latter was the case. At any rate, Franck's father showed some enterprise and boldness in bearding the mighty.

There was only one other award at the Conservatoire for which Franck could enter, the Prix de Rome, that honour won by so many nonentities and so few real geniuses, coveted by the former and despised by the latter (though always accepted), and which was the principal goal of the Conservatoire course. Two obstacles presented themselves. One might have been overcome, but certainly not the latter. In the first place the authorities maintained that Franck was not a Frenchman. In the second, Franck's father decided that things had gone far enough. His son might have won all the prizes and he might have composed three Trios, but there was no tangible profit in them. Having given him a complete musical training it was now time to see results, and César must earn some money. When he had decided that both his sons should 'go in for music', Franck *père* did not mean this composing business. Oh, dear, no. He intended that César should follow the career of a virtuoso pianist with all the attendant glory (and financial gain), and that Joseph, being a weaker limb, should set up as a teacher and organist and earn his living that way. In other words, fame and fortune, especially the latter, were to be the reward of paternal vision, and Reicha's teaching could count for nothing. The young man was removed from the Conservatoire, and made to dedicate and present in person the three Trios to the King of the Belgians. Exactly what he thought would be the result of this gesture is difficult to say. In any case, there was no result, and Franck had to make his way with no distinguished patronage.

However, if the King of the Belgians did not want Franck's Trios, someone else did. The return to Brussels coincided with a visit there by Liszt during the course of a concert tour. Liszt was then at his zenith as a virtuoso pianist and although eleven years older than Franck, he received his friend with every sign of cordiality. Franck produced the Trios. Liszt was so impressed with the completeness and general cohesion of the last movement of the third Trio that he suggested its detachment from the original setting and publication as a separate work. Franck duly detached it, writing another finale for the original Trio; he dedicated the 'new' work to Liszt himself. The matter went further than merely giving advice. Liszt promised to perform it and recommended it to Schuberth, the German publisher. The performance took place, with the third Trio, at Weimar in 1853.

Franck's friends were many and varied. Liszt was his direct antithesis; so was Chabrier with whom a deep friendship was struck up later.

Franck started on the career of a virtuoso pianist, being forced to play things which were all show and little music, and designed entirely to show off the technical prowess of the player and not his musicianship. He set to work to widen the repertoire. Like Liszt, he composed some pieces to suit his own technique which was unique as he had large hands with an enormous stretch. Nothing of any value to piano literature was added, but the method of writing for the instrument in due time exercised an influence on him. An early essay was an *Eclogue*, written in 1842, which includes a startling presage of the later Franck pianism. It was followed by a Duo based on—*God save the King*. This penchant for crowned heads seems to have been an obsession with Franck's father, but there is no record of any idea that Franck should present a copy in person to Queen Victoria.

In 1843 he commenced his first big work, an oratorio *Ruth*.

Belgium apparently proving an unprofitable field, the Franck family moved back to Paris and the composer found that the entire family income was to be derived from his teaching fees and concert engagements. Fortunately music was a fashionable pastime in Paris and Franck found many rich amateurs who were willing to pay him good fees for piano lessons. He still found time to write a quantity of virtuoso music, much of which has been lost and which had no merit save its utility, if we may judge from what remains. His organ success at the Conservatoire had stood him in good stead and he was appointed organist at Notre-Dame-de-Lorette, which gave him further introductions to prospective pupils.

It was at this time that his father's real character was revealed in the fullness of its selfishness and autocracy. He was not in the least interested in anything save his son's progress with the piano. Every hour spent otherwise was completely wasted. He even drew up a table recording the exact time it took Franck to get from pupil to pupil and thence home to the piano. When

Franck expostulated, the reply was 'If you do not obey, it will be your mother who will suffer.' He wrote a short song *L'Ange et l'Enfant* which he showed to his family. They destroyed it. Full of grief, Franck confided his troubles to Mme Desmousseaux whose daughter he taught. Immediately Mme Desmousseaux told him that part of the time in which he was supposed to be teaching her daughter he could spend in composition, if he wished.

Franck's mother stood in awe of her martinet husband, but gradually she gained her son's confidence and gave him the necessary independence of spirit and philosophical outlook which enabled him to pursue his steady course. In all this Franck never complained. He had implicit faith in the guidance of a power above him. He regulated his life on the teachings of the Sermon on the Mount. Although never *un religieux* in the fullest sense of the word (and this is an important point which will be argued later) he was a believer and this faith kept him within due bounds of resignation whenever the paternal oppression became very strong. It must have been a miserable household, dominated by this tyrannical and unsympathetic man, the epitome of so many Victorian fathers.

An event of the most direct significance to Franck took place in 1846 when the completed oratorio *Ruth* was performed at the Conservatoire. Franck made his first contact with hostility. The critics, generally speaking, saw little originality in the work, forgetting that such an element in any case cannot be expected in the first large-scale work by any young composer, and if there had been some striking and individual points, they would have hated them. Criticism in those days was acid, and was written with but the slenderest qualifications. The critics felt it their duty to demolish everything they did not already know. They saw but a pale reflection of Félicien David's *Le Désert*, a symphonic work whose initial mild sensation had not yet worn itself out. They could hardly have seen any reflection at all, for *Le Désert* is deliberately picturesque music, while *Ruth* makes no attempt at delineation. The only credit point appears to have been the extreme simplicity of the expression which was said to have stood the composer well in his approach to the biblical text.

The musicians present thought rather differently. The two loudest in their praise were Meyerbeer and Spontini. This is astonishing. Both these composers were of the flashy type, with their fingers on the theatre. Both relied upon public opinion for their reputation and success. It may have been refreshing to them to enter a world where public opinion was not a matter of consideration to the composer and to listen to music so entirely divorced from their own outlook.

During the space of these years Franck had been writing an orchestral work which, although never published and as far as can be ascertained never performed, is of the highest significance and importance in the history of music. In his book, Vincent d'Indy mentions a work based upon the Sermon on the Mount, and, indeed, gives it this title, suggesting that it was a symphony written as an original part of *Les Béatitudes*. Maurice Emmanuel makes the same mistake. The work in question bears the title *Ce qu'on entend sur la montagne*, but that which was heard on the mountain was the voice of Victor Hugo, not that of Christ.

Here we have a symphonic poem illustrating a verse poem and probably the very first symphonic work of this nature, written before the first of Liszt's. Franck's work will be discussed in some detail in a later chapter because, although it remained unpublished, it is of too great significance to be passed over. Its composition is definitely between 1846 and 1848. James Huneker in his book on Liszt says that Liszt's work on the same subject was sketched in 1833, orchestrated in 1849 and performed in 1853. *Grove*, however, says that it was sketched in 1847 and not published until 1857. Franck never hid his works from his friends. With childlike delight in everything he did, he invariably showed his scores to anyone who was interested, whether famous or obscure—Maurice Emmanuel tells how he found the most elementary of his fellow students with the complete MS score of *Les Béatitudes*. Liszt and Franck were firm friends. Is it beyond the realms of possibility that Franck showed his MS to Liszt and that the latter realized the possibilities of the form? Why should Liszt choose the same subject? Possibly because Franck told him that his work would not be published, in which case there could be no harm in Liszt dealing with the same subject. The evidence, however, does point to Franck's work being the first symphonic poem with a literary basis ever to be composed.

The political situation in Paris was growing steadily worse and one by one Franck's wealthy pupils withdrew to the provinces, leaving him with practically no resources. People react in different ways to these situations. When faced with penury and bankruptcy, Wagner ordered plenty of champagne. Franck faced up to them with more stability. He got married.

On 22nd February 1848 he married the Mlle Desmousseaux whose mother had afforded him a haven of refuge from his terrible father. The wedding took place in the middle of the revolution at Franck's own church of Notre-Dame-de-Lorette. The streets were barricaded at the time, but this was no obstacle and the revolutionaries gravely helped the wedding party over the road blocks.

This marriage, of course, meant a complete rupture with his family. Not that the father objected so much to his son marrying an actress. The bride was a distinguished member of the Théâtre Française and the old man was sufficiently snobbish to appreciate this; but it meant that in future César would pursue his own path and this, the father knew, led away from that of a virtuoso pianist. It was probably the first time that he had ever been defied.

Franck set up his own house, Boulevard Saint Michel 95, now a respectable *Pension en famille*. Franck's wife immediately set herself to humanize her husband. She tried to teach him to dance, but with little success although the bridegroom obligingly composed two trifling little Polkas. She had had to separate herself from the stage, but still liked to go to her old haunts as a spectator; Franck slept through all the performances, remarking that they were a waste of time, otherwise. His theatrical tastes led in the direction of the Opéra Bouffe and he delighted in Offenbach because he said that the operas made him laugh, and he had not done much of this.

The new situation enabled him to catch up with his general education. Franck *père* had frowned violently upon such a thing as reading since it stood in the way of piano practice. Franck *fils* now set to work to read the books which Reicha had quoted and he started on Kant's *The Critique of Pure Reason.* This he described as *amusant,* for which remark he has been blamed and mocked at. The truth is that he did not say 'amusing' and the French word has a distinctly different meaning, but any stick is good enough for the Franck detractors to use. He set aside two hours every day for his own work in this respect and it was now that he established the extraordinary routine to which he stuck for the rest of his life. He never deviated from it. All his music was written between the hours of five and seven each morning, the evenings, and during his eight weeks annual holiday. Often he would turn aside from a lesson to jot down an idea which he would work at later in the day.

It was some time before his system became acclimatized to the arduous life. In 1851 he commenced an opera *Le Valet de Ferme,* the libretto being by two purveyors of such things, Alphonse Royer and Gustave Vaies. Franck worked at it with such zest that he finished it in 1853, but the strain was so great that he suffered a severe breakdown which not only took away all power of composing but made even thought extremely exhausting.

The work was never performed and Franck expressly forbade its publication. Alphonse Royer was appointed Director of the Opéra and one can imagine Franck's delight at what he probably viewed as an act of Divine Providence. Either Royer was a man of the highest integrity or else he viewed the new score with suspicion; anyhow, he declared that his position forbade him ever having a work of his own produced at the Opéra, and there the matter ended. In later years Franck said that he thought so little of the work that no harm was done, except to disappoint him at the time, but the experience gained in writing it was, of course, extremely valuable.

Compensation, however, came along from other directions and he was appointed organist at St-Jean-St-François-au-Marais where Cavaillé-Coll had installed the very latest thing in organs. The delighted Franck described it as 'an orchestra'. Here he worked happily, the urge for composition returning to him in 1858. He was appointed choirmaster at St Clothilde and when the appointment of organist fell vacant, he decided to apply for it. Competition was keen and intrigue subtle, but

Franck succeeded as much by his honesty as by his gifts.

Franck remained here until his death. The organ was a big one, far outsizing the modest 'orchestra' of St-Jean-St-François-au-Marais. St Clothilde became famous because of its organist and his finest organ music was composed expressly for the instrument upon which he played music far above the heads of the congregation, who, if truth were to tell, completely failed to appreciate the genius of his extemporizations. The clergy and congregation were often exasperated by the length of his versets to the Magnificat. However, such influence is always subtle and there is no doubt that he made a certain impression on the subconscious minds of his hearers. Round him gathered a crowd of pupils and admirers and the organ loft was a *sanctum sanctorum* every Sunday for those who admired his playing and loved him as a man.

From 1860 to 1862 he composed the *Six Pièces*, which include the *Fantaisie* (in C), the *Pastorale* and the *Prélude, Fugue, et Variation*. This new appointment did not mean any lessening of his routine activities. Every day he would walk from one end of Paris to the other—walk from 95 Boul' Mich to the Rue Las Casas and one gets a good idea of the mileage covered more than once each Sunday alone. Fortunately he had a very strong constitution and 'the exercise did him good'. He was now a happy man. Whatever worries he had he met with a philosophical resignation. His needs were simple and he loved the company of his friends and pupils. He was *free* to live his own life.

In 1866 Franck had the supreme pleasure of welcoming his old friend Liszt to St Clothilde. Franck offered to play Liszt's *Ad nos* fugue, but the visitor insisted on Franck extemporizing and then playing the *Six Pièces*. On leaving the church, Liszt invoked the name of Johann Sebastian Bach. Nothing could have pleased Franck more because he had been nurtured by Reicha on Bach's music and the compliment he accepted with a beaming smile of incredulity.

The sight of two such opposite types as Franck and Liszt could have been equalled only by the sight of Franck and Chabrier who became close friends just about this time. Chabrier was coarse, ebullient, and exceedingly 'hearty'. In a letter written from Spain, he did not enthuse upon the ancient buildings and traditions of Spain as much as he did over the way the Spanish women 'swung their bottoms' when walking in the streets, this being their normal gait. One can imagine Chabrier telling Franck this in order to watch his face. Franck had a keen sense of humour and was by no means a prude (albeit his sense of the proprieties was well developed) and we can hear his chuckle of delight. Living only in Belgium and France, Franck had no chance of comparing the habits of other countries although there exists an interesting account of his frequent visits to England after his marriage, to stay with some relatives of his wife at Streatham Hill.

He came over as a visitor; nothing more. He attended the Temple Church and Westminster Abbey, delighting in the anthems of Goss and Wesley, and the Anglican Chant. This entirely refutes the legend of his Roman Catholic bigotry which has become part and parcel of the legend of spirituality. He had some curious friends. Brinley Richards and Scotson Clark were the strangest. The latter had studied in Paris and wrote his famous *Marche aux Flambeaux* for a ceremony in honour of the Prince Imperial. Time pressed, so Franck copied out the band parts in one night. In this march he detected a close resemblance to those of Meyerbeer. He attended a Handel Festival which thrilled him, and he acquired a love for the anthems and motets of Tallis, Byrd, and Purcell. The Handel Festival impelled him to ask permission to see Queen Victoria's collection of Handel MSS. The animal in him was satisfied by lunch at the Cock Tavern in the Strand with Dr E. J. Hopkins and dinner at the Café Royal in Regent Street with Scotson Clark. He deputized for Meyer-Lutz at the Roman Catholic Church of St. George, Southwark, and steps were taken to persuade him to judge at an Eisteddfod and to join the staff at Scotson Clark's London Organ School. He is described as 'crackling with wit', altogether rather trying to live with. He returned to France with an intense admiration for Defoe, Fielding, Scott, and Dickens, whom he read in translation.

So wrote the late Andrew de Ternant in the *Musical Times* and in *The Choir*. Without in any way doubting the veracity of this intriguing story, it is impossible to find any corroborating evidence. Franck's son, Georges, was married to Miss Monica Dobson in the Church of Our Lady Star of the Sea at Greenwich on 25th September 1877. Did Franck come over for this ceremony? The certificate was witnessed by Robert Dobson and 'Germain Franck', the composer's second son. Of course, it is possible that Franck played the organ for this ceremony, but, again, there is no confirmation or evidence.

Hopkins makes no mention of Franck in his memoirs—but, then, why should he? Who was Franck? Simply the organist of a church in Paris of nowhere near the standing of the Temple in London. Influential organ lofts always have been invaded by organists of all kinds, anxious to 'try the organ' (do parsons make a habit of 'trying the pulpit' when they visit churches?). Franck had no standing as a composer in France, and French music was not esteemed very highly in England at that time. Hopkins possibly saw in Franck 'just another organist', who was a genial fellow but not worthy of mention.

However, John Hinton, his English pupil, makes no mention of an English visit in his little pamphlet; surely this would have been duly entered up as a great event.

Franck thought Handel ponderous and dull. Would he have been likely to sit through three or four hours of him at a gargantuan festival? Search in the Public Records Office and elsewhere reveals no mention or trace of any application received from Streatham Hill for a 'M César Franck' to visit the Royal Library and there is no record of such a permit being issued. Had it arrived too late, and Franck had repeated his visit, surely it would have been valid for the next occasion?

He was not in the least interested in the music of the sixteenth century, as Henri Expert testifies. Why this enthusiasm for Tallis and Byrd? Further, Franck could not afford to go to Bayreuth. How could he afford to come here, which was a much more expensive journey? Let us concede the fact that if he came for his son's wedding, he saved up for it—but there is not the slightest evidence for certain that he ever came here at all, and his granddaughter maintains that he never did; since she lived with her grandmother for thirty years after Franck's death—she was eight years old when that took place—is it not possible that something would have been said about it during the telling of family stories and the recounting of her grandfather's life?

One hates to spoil a good thing, and if only there were some little evidence to back up Mr de Ternant's story, it would be delightful.

Franck now began to compose more quickly and on a consistently big scale. In 1865 he wrote an oratorio *La Tour de Babel* which he did not allow to be published, but the time was nearing when he would be able to embark on his life's ambition, *Les Béatitudes*. This he commenced in 1869. The next year saw the beginning of the Franco-Prussian war. Franck found it difficult to keep his mind on his music. Although a Walloon by birth, his heart was French, and in France. He found the situation very distressing, mentally as well as physically. His house was in the direct line of fire, but nothing would induce him to move. On the contrary, his quiet confidence was an inspiration to others. His pupils were mostly of military age and joined the colours, but a certain number were in the Paris garrison and continued their lessons in spite of the siege.

Henri Duparc tells a revealing story of Franck during the siege of Paris. Duparc's grandmother had been evacuated from Paris and had given Franck the run of all her coal and wood. Franck found some of his wife's relatives who had been what we should call bombed-out. He immediately took them to live with him in his house on the Boul' Mich. Duparc visited his grandmother's house quite by chance one day when on leave and saw the astonishing sight of Franck and his son running along the street with a bucket of fuel in each hand. He followed them along the route from the Rue Saint Honoré, along the Rue Cambon to the Boulevard Saint Michel where Franck explained that he had a few friends staying with him.

Duparc asked him how he managed to feed so many when there was such a food shortage. Franck drew attention to some large boxes of chocolate and told Duparc that every day the household had a big meal of it, but, of course, 'it is necessary to cook it'—hence the transport by hand of buckets of coal and wood across Paris.

The patriotic soul of Franck was stirred by a poem published in a Paris newspaper by an unknown author 'B. de L. Capitaine de la Garde Mobile', 'I am Paris; Queen of all Cities.' His pupils found him in a state of high excitement over this and he put

31

aside *Les Béatitudes* in order to set it for voice and orchestra. The detractors who sneer at Franck's apparent lack of education and literary judgment (as if it was his fault) seize upon this work, usually without knowing either the poem or the music. Neither is very great, but neither is intended to be so and at any rate what in ordinary circumstances would be banal acquires an added dignity in extraordinary conditions. Is Elgar's *Carillon* a great work and is the poem anything but a cry from the heart of Belgium? Vincent d'Indy gives *Paris* as unpublished but this was rectified in 1917. D'Indy omits mention of a setting of Victor Hugo's *Patria*, which is vastly inferior to *Paris*.

In 1871 Franck, in company with a singer named Bussine, and Camille Saint-Saëns, founded the 'Société Nationale de Musique'. Franck's pupil Alexis de Castillon became the first secretary. The basic idea was to perform new French music, no matter to what school it belonged. For many years it was the tilting ground of opposing factions and most of the leading French composers received their baptism of fire and hisses at its concerts.

Ruth was performed for the second time at the Cirque des Champs-Elysées. This resulted in a complete turn-about on the part of many of the critics who despised it on its previous performance. The critic who admired Franck's simplicity seemed to have forgotten that he had heard it before and proclaimed it a 'masterpiece'. However he qualified his praise with the remark that it recalled Méhul's *Joseph* by reason of its simplicity.

Chapter Three

1872-1890-1922

A PLACID life is sometimes stunned by some kind of shock, either pleasant or unpleasant, and those who work quietly and independently, keeping their activities to their own immediate circle, receive intimation in no uncertain manner that 'someone has heard of them'. François Benoist, Franck's original organ teacher at the Conservatoire, resigned on the score of age. He was, indeed, very old. Massenet described his fifty years (which dated from the time of Louis XVIII) at the Conservatoire, in witty terms, saying that Benoist had 'killed under him three kings, an emperor, and two republics'! Maurice Emmanuel says that he had not changed his methods of teaching since the time of his original appointment. To everyone's surprise, and Franck himself was no less astonished, Franck was offered the vacant appointment at the Conservatoire. For many years it was not known how or why this happened, but eventually, on the occasion of the unveiling of the memorial in the grounds of St Clothilde on 22nd October 1904, Théodore Dubois disclosed the whole matter. Dubois said 'When the appointment of Organ Professor fell vacant I went immediately to find my master Ambroise Thomas, the Director, and said to him "There is only one man today really worthy of filling this appointment. It is César Franck." He answered me thus: "It is true", and he appointed him. I say this because Ambroise Thomas was reported to be hostile to Franck. This was not so. Ambroise Thomas was a man of the highest intelligence, of an outlook too great for this to be the case, and I affirm that he appreciated the exceptional merits of Franck.'

c

Franck himself never knew who was responsible for the appointment, but that did not worry him. He entered upon his duties with the utmost enthusiasm and surrounded himself with a circle of friends and pupils, thereby bringing upon his head the enmity and jealousy, to say nothing of the suspicion and fear, of his colleagues. Of this he was blissfully unaware. It was always possible for students to attend lessons given by professors other than their own, as 'listeners-in'. A pupil of Leo Delibes wished to join the organ class in this capacity. Delibes wrote the parents the following letter in 1887.

Your son wishes to attend the organ class. I can see no objection to this were the professor more reserved in the advice he gives to the pupils in other classes. M Franck, for whom I have the highest esteem, has dangerous tendencies; he tries to make everybody share his tastes. He opposes those of his colleagues whose duty it is to lead their pupils to [the Prix de] Rome. Your son should avoid such subversive teaching.

One of these 'listeners-in' was Georges Bizet who delighted in the classes because they were so different from those he normally attended.

Franck was the only musician in Paris capable of teaching symphonic composition. All kinds of Conservatoire pupils asked to 'stand-in' at his lessons both at the Conservatoire and at his house to see what they were like, duly reporting to their own professors. Franck behaved with scrupulous integrity towards the Conservatoire and his colleagues, refusing to take on Pierre de Bréville until he had completed his Course. The narrowness of the Conservatoire can be shown by M Pierre de Bréville's story of how he produced a copy of *Parsifal* and his composition professor sternly forbade him even to bring it into the building again. Orchestration was not taught there and students had to study it either outside or on their own.

Franck as a teacher of both organ and composition was a man of inspiring vitality. He was ruthless in his criticisms, but he always gave his reasons, and was suitably encouraging when necessary. The organ was not the splendid affair such as exists in the present building. It had two manuals and was sixty years old. It had sufficed Benoist, and Franck recognized it as an old friend. Nevertheless, despite its shortcomings, it served some dis-

tinguished Paris organists. Franck excelled in extemporization
and would work himself into a perfect frenzy of excitement.
'First find a beautiful countersubject.' He would immediately
'find' two or three himself if the pupil was overcome with nerves.
'*Listen* to me,' he would say, 'But come to St Clothilde on Sunday. I will *show* you.' He taught them music as distinct from
teaching them merely the subject, and he believed in example.

As a composition teacher he was supreme. He always referred
to the great masters. 'See how Beethoven gets out of the very
same difficulty' he would say. Over and over again he would
play a passage which at first sight offended him until eventually
he would say 'I like it'. 'They would not allow you to do that at
the Conservatoire, but I like it' was another dictum of his. He
not only inspired his pupils with a love for music, but he inspired
them with a love for himself.

The year 1872, therefore, marked a turning point in Franck's
career. He put *Les Béatitudes* aside and wrote an oratorio in two
parts, *Redemption*. It was performed at a Maundy Thursday
'concert spirituel' by Edouard Colonne. Unfortunately the succeeding Good Friday Concert consisted of Massenet's *Marie-
Madeleine*, a long oratorio to which Colonne, in his (then) inexperience had to allot most of the rehearsal time. Franck had to
cut out a symphonic interlude between the two parts, but this
was later re-written and its omission did no harm to the work in
question. In spite of the mediocrity of the performance Franck
was quite satisfied, being only too pleased that the work had
been performed at all.

In 1873 he became a naturalized Frenchman.

His life, with the exception of one or two incidents, now became mainly a diary of composition. He worked at *Les Béatitudes*
until 1879, interrupting it to write a new interlude and a male
chorus for *Rédemption* in 1874, while in 1876 he completed the
symphonic poem *Les Eolides*. However, bigger than any of these
works was the great Piano Quintet which he began in 1878 and
finished in 1879. He helped to inaugurate the new organ at the
Trocadéro by composing, in 1878, the *Trois Pièces* which include
the *Cantabile*. The next year his early fourth Trio received its
first performance—it will be remembered as having been written
as far back as 1842. This was another venture of the Société

35

nationale. The Quintet was played by the same Society in 1880. Saint-Saëns was persuaded to play the piano part. Franck was so delighted with the performance that immediately afterwards he went up to Saint-Saëns to thank him, saying that he would like to dedicate the work to him and handing over the original MS as a present. Then followed a shocking display of bad manners. Saint-Saëns made an ugly face, tossed the MS on to the piano, turned on his heel and strode away. Either Franck did not see this, or else he had a finely developed sense of dignity. Years afterwards the MS was picked up in a pile of waste paper by an employee of Pleyel, the piano manufacturer.

Saint-Saëns was utterly impossible in many ways but this behaviour was unforgivable and showed complete lack of breeding. Afterwards he expressed himself as hating the passionate warmth of the work—perhaps it reached a height to which he was unable to climb. The score, however, bore the inscription 'To my friend Camille Saint-Saëns' and that inscription was not erased. That the MS should have been left on the piano was tactless of the pupils of Franck who were present, but an action such as this may well have taken their breath away and perhaps they hurried Franck off before anything could be done. Vincent d'Indy tells the story and there is no reason to doubt its truth because several times Saint-Saëns expressed his hatred of Franck's music, speaking of it in terms of the greatest scorn.

Les Béatitudes had by now reached completion and Franck decided to arrange a private performance in his house which had a room large enough for this kind of activity. The soloists were Conservatoire pupils and the chorus consisted of twenty of Franck's friends. Invitations were issued to the Minister of Fine Arts and the Director of the Conservatoire and of the Opéra. On the day of the performance, message after message of regret came in. A few critics looked in for a short time and then left to cover the first night of a popular operetta. In the end there were only two people in the audience, Edouard Lalo whose reputation as a composer was established and Vincent Jonçières, the composer of an opera *Dimitri* whose subject is the same as *Boris Godunov*. This is Vincent d'Indy's story and it seems rather a dramatization, to say the least. In default of other evidence we must believe it, incredible though it sounds. Knowing the hostility towards Franck, one can well believe it. (Did he send an invitation to Camille Saint-Saëns?) The whole work was not performed again until after Franck's death and the performance established it as a masterpiece—but it could not atone for the early neglect.

However, the Minister of Fine Arts had a conscience, for he did his best to have Franck appointed to the composition class made vacant by the death of Victor Massé; but the Conservatoire authorities overruled him and gave the chair to Ernest Guirard, a composer of light operas and the orchestrator of Offenbach's *Les Contes d'Hoffmann*. Compensation followed, and Franck was made an Officier de l'Académie. His pupils and friends were furious, but Franck himself was quite satisfied, saying that 'they have given me every hope for next year'. It was not till 1885 that he received the honour of Chevalier du Légion d'Honneur and then it was awarded him as a professor of organ who had completed ten years service rather than as a composer. In all fairness it is difficult to see upon what other grounds he could have received it. His works were few in number, comparatively speaking, and he was by no means a regular name in concert programmes. He did not compose operas or operettas, and did not teach composition at the Conservatoire. There was but one way of awarding it, and that as Professor of Organ. Any attempt to give it him as a composer who had added to the glory of France would have met with furious opposition.

Franck was now working hard. *Rébecca*, a scena for soli, chorus, and orchestra, appeared in 1881 and the symphonic poem *Le Chasseur maudit* in 1882; in the same year he began the opera *Hulda*. The next few years were of the utmost importance. Franck had noticed that very few major works for piano had been produced by the Société nationale, and decided that he would like to apply some of the old forms to that instrument, bringing them into line with up-to-date technique, and thus producing something as broad as Beethoven. The result was first of all the symphonic poem *Les Djinns* for piano and orchestra, based on Victor Hugo's poem. This was followed by an extended work for piano the *Prélude, Choral, et Fugue*. Intended as a prelude and fugue only in a rather elaborate style of Bach, the chorale was an afterthought, as it were. It was performed by the

Société nationale on 24th January 1885, by Saint-Saëns who as usual hated it and described the fugue as 'not a fugue'. Franck finished *Hulda* and composed the complete *Variations symphoniques*, following up with the Violin Sonata and the *Prélude, Aria et Final* for piano in 1886, beginning the Symphony at the same time—not a bad year's work. During this year he was able to welcome Liszt to Paris for the last time when the aged composer attended a performance of his *Graner Messe* at St Eustache.

In 1886 there occurred the great split in the Société nationale. Vincent d'Indy and others from the Schola Cantorum decided that the scope should be widened to include other than French music. This enraged Saint-Saëns, who had been one of the founders and who saw in the influence something aimed at the very roots and intentions of the society.

The *Prélude, Aria, et Final* was duly finished and *Psyché* was started in 1887. The latter was produced by the Société nationale in 1888 and again in February 1890.

The *Prélude, Aria, et Final* was performed for the first time on 12th May 1888 (*not* 1898 as stated in the English translation of M Alfred Cortot's *French Piano Music*) at a concert of the Société nationale. The critics hated it. M Cortot quotes two of them, M Boutarel of the *Menestrel* and M Julien Torchet of the *Monde Artiste*. The former laconically dismissed the work as 'a piece by M Franck, long and tedious'. The latter spread himself a little more. He said that he preferred to respect Franck rather than to listen to him. He commended him to a M Camille Bellaifue who previously had suggested a list of musicians 'who are boring though still living'. He described Franck as 'really no more than a competent professor'. This may be a natural reaction when we consider the piano literature of the period, but the pianos were not quite what they are now, and perhaps if the two critics had heard the work played on one of our pianos they might have got a better impression.

Some of Franck's friends decided that a 'Franck Festival' was overdue and having collected the necessary financial guarantee, gave a long programme at the Cirque d'Hiver on 30th January 1887. It was conducted by Jules Pasdeloup and by Franck himself. The works performed were *Le Chasseur maudit*, the *Variations symphoniques*, and the second part of *Ruth* in the

first half, under Pasdeloup, and in the second half Franck conducted the March and Air de Ballet from *Hulda* and the third
and eighth *Béatitudes*. As usual, the performances appear to have
been very mediocre. Pasdeloup was too old to undertake such
an advanced programme and the *Variations* ended in a breakdown (we can guess where and why). Like most composers,
Franck was a bad conductor of his own works and the two
Béatitudes suffered accordingly. He himself was perfectly satisfied. He had written the music because he felt he had to, and
his friends had very generously organized a concert in his
honour. Why regret what happened at a concert intended primarily as a gesture of friendship?

He essayed another opera in 1888, *Ghisèle*, but although completed in composition it was only sketched in as regards the orchestration. This was finished later by five of his pupils. It was
not performed until 1896.

In 1889 the Symphony received its first performance at the
Société des Concerts du Conservatoire, under Garcin, and was
greeted with indignation and fury. It was on a serious plane
quite out of line with the prevailing thought in Paris; further, it
used a cor anglais. The latter seems innocent enough, but its use
was pounced on by all and sundry. One critic stated that it
settled definitely the fact that Franck's symphony was not a
symphony at all 'whatever else you may call it'. No less an
authority than the composer of *The Bloody Nun* and *Faust* ponti-
ficated to a circle of sycophants that the work was 'an affirma-
tion of incompetence pushed to the length of a dogma', whatever
that may have meant. Another critic asked 'Why play this symphony here? Who is this M Franck? A professor of harmonium,
I believe.' Ambroise Thomas, who always maintained that 'M
Franck is too chromatic', shook his head sadly and failed to see
how a symphony which passed through so many keys in so short
a time could be described as being in the key of D minor.

One loud approving voice sounded above the din of dis-
approval. Chabrier admired the work and said so with his customary vehemence. Of Franck's colleagues it is but fair to say
that Massenet, Guiraud, and Dubois stood up for him. And
Franck himself? His wife had not dared go to the concert as she
was terrified of the probable result. On opening the door of his

house Franck said 'It sounded well, just as I thought it would.'

Franck finished what was to be his first real success, the String Quartet, but it was not performed till the following year. D'Indy says that the pupils noticed a quantity of string quartets lying about Franck's study and guessed what was afoot. Before embarking on this hazardous travail, Franck read through every quartet by Beethoven, Schubert and Brahms with the greatest attention.

It was performed by the Société nationale in 1890 and was a veritable triumph. Franck was recalled over and over again, but he could not realize that the applause was for himself as well as for the players. 'There, they are beginning to understand me at last.' After a successful Festival at Tournai, organized by Eugène Ysaÿe (who played the violin sonata), Franck returned to his routine and to his last music, the three organ Chorals and what he hoped would be a hundred versets to the Magnificat.

In May that year he met with an accident. On his way to his pupil Paul Brand he was knocked down by an omnibus. Pneumonia set in and he retired to bed. The Société nationale played the Quartet at its annual general meeting but Franck was unable to be present. He lingered until 8th November, dying peacefully.

He was buried in the cemetery at Montrouge, his body being transferred later to Montparnasse. Vincent d'Indy paints a gloomy picture of the funeral. Apparently all those who should have been present stayed away and only his friends accompanied him. The pall-bearers included Delibes, Franck's pupil Henri Dallier, and Saint-Saëns, the last-named after some persuasion. Ambroise Thomas according to d'Indy was suddenly taken ill and there were no Conservatoire or Beaux Arts representatives. This is altogether incredible because Guiraud, Massenet and Dubois, to mention only three of his colleagues, were on the best of terms with him. Emmanuel Chabrier represented the Société nationale and delivered the customary oration.

His death passed practically unnoticed in this country. The *Athenaeum* included a short paragraph, quoting *Ruth* as his most representative work, and then only on hearsay. The first edition of *Grove* relegated him to the supplement.

As early as the next year, however, things began to be differ-

ent. On 15th, 16th and 18th June 1891 the complete *Les Béatitudes* was performed at Dijon under the Abbé Maître, in connection with the sixth centenary celebrations of St Bernard.
This enterprise on the part of an amateur was remarkable. The
Abbé collected his singers from Paris and assembled round him
an orchestra. The performers were drawn from every stratum of
society and included the leading professional musicians as well
as amateurs. Rehearsals went on consistently for three weeks. As
a result Edouard Colonne was persuaded to give a similar performance at the Châtelet, in Paris. Nowadays such an enterprise in a small provincial city organized by an amateur enthusiast would be spoken of as remarkable, and that the capital
should follow suit, even more so. In those days it was almost a
miracle.

Fourteen years later the memorial in the grounds of St Clothilde was unveiled with due pomp and circumstance, and this
ceremony was attended by all the institutions which had been
absent from the funeral. The Directors of both the Conservatoire and Beaux Arts each delivered an oration which sounded
as if Franck had been acknowledged to the full during his lifetime. The Institut, however, could not send a representative as
Franck had not been elected a member. His name had been
suggested in 1880, together with those of Saint-Saëns, Delibes,
Guiraud, Lalo and Félix Clémont. Franck does not seem to have
received any votes.

The centenary of his birth was celebrated in a completely
fitting manner. There was a concert at the Paris Opéra on
7th March to herald the handing over of a monument to the
city of Liége on behalf of the French musicians. The programme
consisted of

> LE CHASSEUR MAUDIT
> VARIATIONS SYMPHONIQUES (Arthur de Greef)
> RÉDEMPTION
> 4th and 8th BÉATITUDES

and Chausson's *Poème* for violin and orchestra, played by
Jacques Thibaud.

The conducting was divided up among Franck's pupils and
friends, the honours going to Gabriel Pierné, Paul Vidal, Rhené-

Baton, Camille Chevillard, Guy Ropartz, Henri Rabaud, Philippe Gaubert, and Vincent d'Indy.

The monument was unveiled in the presence of Elizabeth, Queen of the Belgians, being handed over by Henri Rabaud, and the ceremony was followed by a complete performance of *Les Béatitudes* under Sylvain Dupuis, the Director of the Liége Conservatoire.

At two concerts on 9th and 10th December given by the Colonne Society under Gabriel Pierné the following works were played :

> SYMPHONY
> VARIATIONS SYMPHONIQUES (Tatiana de Jangevitch)
> LES BÉATITUDES
> RÉDEMPTION
> PSYCHÉ

The city of Paris organized a festival at the Châtelet on 20th December, again under Gabriel Pierné, at which

> LA MARSEILLAISE
> LA BRABANÇONNE
> SOLEIL (Chorus and Orchestra)
> SYMPHONY
> RÉDEMPTION
> PARIS

were played.

In Strasbourg, Guy Ropartz conducted on 18th December a concert consisting of

> SYMPHONY
> NOCTURNE ET PROCESSION (Mme Martinelli)
> RÉDEMPTION

Among the smaller celebrations, Cesare Galeotti and the Capet quartet played the Quartet, Quintet, and Violin Sonata at the Conservatoire on 15th March, while a particularly interesting 'concert spirituel' was given at St Clothilde on 31st March, the organists being Dallier, Mahout, Tournemire, Marty, Gigout, Pierné, and Galeotti. At this concert the 'Musiciens de la Renaissance' sang a *Salut* under the direction of Jules Meunier.

On the 19th of November the commemorative plaque on Boulevard St Michel 95 was unveiled and in the evening there was a concert at the Schola Cantorum.

In this country the centenary celebrations took the form mainly of innumerable organ recitals. Truth to tell, the organ works were the only ones which were familiar here. As an orchestral composer Franck's name was by no means generally known and the orchestral works had not become established— *Les Éolides*, for example, does not appear to have been performed until 1914. The leading musical journals, however, published articles which made a very fair assessment from limited knowledge.

One other celebration may be mentioned. On 22nd June 1939 the 60th anniversary of *Les Béatitudes* fell due. There was another 'concert spirituel' at St Clothilde when Charles Tournemire played the third Choral and *Pièce Héroïque*, and Alfred Cortot conducted part of *Les Béatitudes* and *Rédemption*.

Chapter Four

General Characteristics
of his music

IT is usual to consider the works in detail before drawing up an assessment. With Franck, a highly stylized composer, this is not feasible and the examination of his general characteristics must take place before the works are considered. Such a process will serve to elucidate what follows and need not be thought of as putting the cart before the horse.

Every composer with individuality has his salient features of technique, his own particular way of saying things. It is only copyists who can tell us nothing about themselves because they have nothing to say. A composer's true personality can shine out in his music. Creative work does not always go by contraries. The old story of the organist whose playing sent his hearers to Heaven every Sunday but who beat his wife regularly every week-day does not necessarily apply to composers although there are isolated instances—not of wife-beating, but of a mild man like Roussel, for example, whose musical violence was utterly at variance with his personality. This is probably more apparent with French composers than with those of any other race, for it is a national characteristic of the French that they are not restrained in their behaviour and conversation. When a Frenchman is down, he is very much down, but when up, usually terrific. A Frenchman does not fear sentiment. An Englishman would run a mile rather than show that he has the slightest feelings of this nature; on the other hand, if he is elated, he has no hesitation in showing it. A British composer feels almost naked and ashamed if the pathos of a work is pointed out to him. His French colleague welcomes it.

There is a danger that being so far removed from the Latin temperament we see more than really exists. This is certainly the case in the average regard of Franck, although Franck was by no means a pure Latin. Without in any way entering upon a discussion of racial characteristics, we can say that the Walloon in Franck counteracted the Latin, and those who are emphatic on his Frenchness have never been able to convince others of the truth of their opinion. It may be strange that the salvation of French music lay in the hands of a Belgian, but in this country we have not forsworn the influence of Germans, from whatever provinces they may have come. Handel was no more an Englishman than was Franck a Frenchman, while Mendelssohn influenced music and musicians here to an incalculable extent, and at a time when the situation was very bad with our own native composers. It took the sobering influence of a Walloon to pull French music together from the effervescence in which it was bubbling. As we have seen in our first chapter, the position of French music was parlous because society had not allowed it to be taken seriously as a national culture.

The utter seriousness of Franck's purpose was quite unique at the time and altogether out of the picture. Had he proceeded along traditional lines, he would have been just another composer, perhaps of the calibre of Cherubini, a mere historical figure. However, Reicha saw to this.

Before considering his technique, let us for a moment see from the contemporary programmes what music he is likely to have heard during his student days. It was obligatory for all students to attend the rehearsals as well as all the concerts taking place in the Conservatoire; this was part of the training. The principal concerts were those of the Société des Concerts du Conservatoire founded in 1828 by Cherubini and Habeneck. The latter, originally a violin student at the Conservatoire, was conductor at the Paris Opéra. The inception of the Society was from him, and was due to his discovery of Beethoven whose works to date Habeneck performed in Paris before anyone else had heard of them. Between 1837 and 1841, the period of Franck's studentship, the programmes included the Mass in D, the Symphonies as they became available, and many of the Overtures. Other composers heard were Handel (*Judas Maccabeus*, *Samson*, and *Messiah* of the oratorios and a few of the operas, including *Alexander*), many symphonies of Haydn, some Motets and *The Creation*, many symphonies by Mozart, the *Requiem*, and extracts from *Don Giovanni*, and the Overture to *The Magic Flute*. Of the French composers, Rameau and Méhul, and, later, Lulli, but always Cherubini by virtue of his position as Director of the Conservatoire and President of the Society.

After his return to Paris in 1843 Franck continued to hear as much as he could. Habeneck had widened the repertoire as time went on, including the *Stabat Mater* of Pergolesi, *The Ruins of Athens* by his beloved Beethoven, and the Mendelssohn Violin Concerto. Bach was a closed book at these concerts as his works were for the main part unpublished.

Franck also attended the Opéra and probably the first work he heard was Berlioz's *Benvenuto Cellini* produced in 1838. Meyerbeer was the king in this field, closely followed by Halévy. Rossini was beginning to fade after *Guillaume Tell* in 1829 and Spontini, the one time absolute monarch of the stage, had vanished altogether. Halévy's now forgotten opera *La Juive* played an influential part with composers of its period and the other names which appeared on the bills were Auber, Donizetti, Niedermeyer, and Adam. One other could be seen in a castrated version. Weber's *Der Freischütz* appeared in 1841 in a form never imagined by its composer, and called *Robin des Bois*.

Franck himself was nourished on the later Beethoven and such works of Bach as came his way via Reicha after the revelation of the *St Matthew Passion* at Berlin, under Mendelssohn, in 1829. Wagner had not penetrated to any degree and although Franck grew enthusiastic as time went on, he never allowed his own individuality to be swamped.

Such was the musical background of Franck and from this backcloth he made his own tradition and that of a certain facet of French music. It remains to be seen how faithfully he remained true to himself.

The component parts of the Franck technique are a warmth of harmony, a sense of counterpoint within the context and a rhythmic vitality which does not always avoid vulgarity. While Liszt may be said to have immortalized the diminished seventh and Brahms the sixth, Franck certainly played an equal part with the dominant ninth—and here let us remember that it is Debussy who is usually credited with this venture. It was Franck, not Debussy, who formulated and practised the theory that in order to get a free music every chord must be considered a concord and a complete entity in itself. However, he treated the mass of sound with a strong feeling for progression and tonality. Debussy was never altogether happy about Franck. The latter's sense of and insistence on modulation disturbed him. 'Modulate, modulate' cried the enthusiastic Franck to Debussy when the latter was extemporizing. 'Why should I' replied Debussy 'when I am perfectly happy in this key?' and forthwith changed his professor. Franck was not one of those 'teachers' who say to the pupil that if that is what he wants, well, then, he will have to have it.

It is difficult to imagine Debussy sitting at the feet of Franck at the Conservatoire because the two outlooks were in direct opposition. Franck applied 'impressionism' to classical harmony. Debussy avoided the latter because it did not interest him and he did not feel that way. Nevertheless, his early *Fantaisie* for piano and orchestra is extremely under the influence of Franck both harmonically (in a few respects) and certainly formally. For this reason Debussy repudiated the work, but whatever his attitude may have been, he realized that in Franck he could find his own solutions and his writings speak of him with the greatest respect and admiration.

Franck's harmonic sense was limited, but his chromaticism is always in the context, and is always tender if frequently sentimental. His insistence on tonality at any price, even at the expense of key relationship was dictated by the thought. When he wanted to be bright he chose sharp keys, when sad, flat; hence the dreadful muddle of the organ *Final* where the stereotyped notation leads him into the key of A sharp major—an enharmonic change would have eased the situation at once and given the player no anxious moments. Both Saint-Saëns and Ambroise Thomas complained of his chromaticism, the former with venom, the latter with regret. Thomas simply could not see it.

47

'How can you describe a symphony as in the key of D minor
when the principal theme at the ninth bar goes into D flat, at
the tenth C flat, at the twenty-first F sharp minor, at the twenty-
fifth B flat minor, at the twenty-sixth C minor, at the thirty-
ninth E flat major, at the forty-ninth F minor?' It must be
agreed that this was rather a lot for the composer of *Mignon* to
swallow, but it does not prove hostility. It will be remembered
that Dubois repudiated the accusation that Thomas was hostile
to Franck. The Franck admirers have always had the unhappy
knack of seeing hostility in any sign of adverse comment. At any
rate, most of this is fact and not criticism, the only touch of the
latter being the first question.

Franck would never have got out a 'drill' for emotion (I came
across a book once which purported to give a list of chords for
every emotional crisis—'Everybody's Book of Passion' in fact!).
His key changes were all dictated by the feeling of the music.
When he modulated or simply passed through a series of keys,
he did so usually by falling thirds. His fondness for suddenly
changing the mode from major to minor, and vice versa, for a
bar or two was evidenced at an early age (see Ex. 11, page
62). This is characteristic of the Quintet.

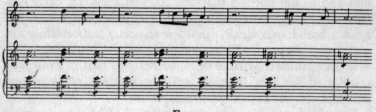

Ex. 1

It is one of the most striking instances of the influence of
Reicha.

He thought contrapuntally, not in the manner of Bach, but
in the matter of instinctively writing themes in double counterpoint. The organ *Cantabile* is a remarkable example of this, the
bass and treble alternating in positions but never giving the
feeling of being forced. His melodies are very often in two or
four bar phrases and he placed great store on appoggiaturas.
His themes grow. He formed the easy habit of making an inci-

dental fragment the constituent part of a completely new phrase.
Let us take two such themes and notice how this is done.

Ex. 2

The sequence at 'A' is engendered at the second bar of the
phrase. This falling succession of thirds itself engenders 'B',
while the sequence at 'C' is founded upon the second and third
bars of 'B'. Observe also the spaciousness of the whole theme,
the way in which its intensity is built up by means of wider and
wider leaps.

Ex. 3

As Ex. 2 was disjunct, so is this conjunct, an 'infinite melody'.
The germinal semitone at 'A' controls the whole progress of the
theme, and the semitonal descent at 'B' is made the salient
opening of the second phrase.

Another feature is the slight variant of a two bar figure as in
the second subject of the Symphony (first movement).

Ex. 4

D

An examination of the pencilled sketches of *Les Éolides* shows that he sketched out the melody first, paying scant attention to the harmony unless he wanted a definite harmonic figure. The themes grew out of each other with this process, and it is obvious how the question of key became of secondary importance. He went simply where the melodic contour dictated, and he took infinite pains over the matter. He crossed out at least two pages of his preliminary sketch, but unfortunately he did this too thoroughly to allow us to see exactly what he discarded, and why. Sequence he used freely, and this often gives a feeling of immobility. The music in these instances goes round and round rather than onwards and onwards. He is fond of centralizing a theme round one note. He leaves a note to return to it, widening the interval as in Ex. 4 and in the *Pastorale* for organ. Nevertheless he obtains considerable freedom of movement by syncopation, as in the finale of the Symphony.

It all sounds spontaneous, but there is sometimes a lack of discrimination and self-criticism. The codas are good examples of this, particularly those in the Symphony, the *Variations symphoniques*, the Violin Sonata and the first Choral. Here we have commonplace triumphant endings which are satisfactory in themselves as endings, but could have been of much higher quality with a little thought. There is clarity throughout and he never overlaid his lines with extraneous counterpoints and decorations which attract the attention from the real matter in hand.

He did not paint pictures or illustrate stories in everything he wrote and he may be one of the few replies to those who maintain that there is no such thing as 'abstract' music. It is difficult to say why such and such a work sounds 'inspired' when there is nothing concrete to point to, and this indicates that Franck was a great genius as well as an architect. There are a lot of composers to whom one can point and say that their technical equipment is superb but that they lack a real musical impulse. Max Reger and Vincent d'Indy are cases in point. The driving force behind Franck, therefore, was one of sheer musical expression and it is obvious that he is at his weakest when attempting to delineate something—*Le Chasseur maudit*, for example.

He knew the value of silences. 'Let in the air' and 'Let the music breathe'; so did he exhort his pupils. The detractors point to the organ as the origin and reason for his haltings, and the necessity for stop changing and the clearing up of echo. Nevertheless, these pauses are dramatic and herald the achievement of climaxes.

Contrapuntally conceived within itself, his music is never devised even if well designed and built. In a world singularly devoid of musical solidity and thought, his music stood out in sharp relief.

His pianism was something peculiar to himself. Pianists find many awkwardnesses; stretches of tenths in the left hand and widely spaced arpeggii cause the hands to lose all their instinctive positions, as do the foibles of Brahms. Nevertheless, everything is playable, but not everyone has Franck's enormous compass. He used the piano pianistically and never showily. A virtuoso out for applause will find few openings in Franck because it was always the music which lay pre-eminent in his mind. No one has written for piano in this manner since Franck.

He had a certain flair for orchestration and this makes the flatness of the symphony all the more remarkable. When scoring the orchestral part of a choral work he was never venturesome and the instrumental accompaniments are always subservient to the choral. Orchestration as a subject in itself was not taught at the Conservatoire and therefore he had to pick it up with the aid of the harmony treatise of Reicha and his own reading of the available scores of the period. There are, therefore, no orchestral stunts, no excitable arpeggii or other passage work. The instruments are each and all used rationally. The delicacy of *Les Éolides* is essentially French.

As a song writer, probably *La Procession* is the only one which will survive. There is nothing strikingly individual about any of the others. *Paris* is a document which should not be forgotten however.

His church music is remarkably feeble. He was quite ignorant of the origin of plainsong and the word 'Solesmes' meant nothing to him. What little he knew of Palestrina did not appeal to him. All the music of the 16th century left him cold and when Henri Expert told him of some plans he had in this direction,

Franck hardly listened to him. He had to write the repertoire for St Clothilde and here he was out of his depth. This is in no sense derogatory to his genius: it is not given to everyone to be J. S. Bach.

He lived in the late works of Beethoven, the quartets and sonatas. His lack of concern over key relationships has the authority of the Op. 110. Méhul, Bach, Beethoven and Schubert were his ideals. Handel he considered pompous and grandiloquent.

Of his contemporaries, Liszt held the highest place. He always wanted to go to Bayreuth but it did not occur to anyone to make him a present of the trip. Instead he was forced to study the works in score since his duties as a church organist often prevented him from attending concerts. Of *Tristan und Isolde* he thought highly but he never allowed himself to be swamped by the Wagnerian incubus. He had a certain opinion of his own works. In the paper *L'Université* of November 1890 Henri Cochin tells that one day Franck met one of his most unpretentious pupils in the street. The pupil told him that he had just studied *Tristan* in detail and waxed eloquent on the subject. Franck also spoke eloquently on the work and when saying good-bye to the pupil remarked 'And now do me a favour. After *Tristan* take the score of *Les Béatitudes*: what Wagner has done for human love, I have done for divine.' Berlioz's *Beatrice et Benedict* called forth his admiration but he regretted the bad counterpoint and false basses of *Faust*. Gounod he detested, but where opera was concerned he admired Massenet, Méhul's *Joseph*, and Saint-Saëns's *Samson et Dalila*, considering the latter one of the finest dramatic works in existence. It was a pity that the facile composer could find no place for Franck, in return. Alkan, a composer all but unknown in this country, was another of his favourites.

It is significant that his violin sonata, piano quintet and string quartet were his greatest successes. His bent was particularly suited for chamber music and the three examples rank with the highest in all music.

On the matter of form he placed the highest importance, and we must devote some considerable space to its consideration because his name stands for everything that is logical and sound in this respect:

52

Franck is always associated with the cyclic form. The basic idea of this form is to weld the movements of a symphony or sonata into a homogeneous whole by the use of the initial material. This can be done in several ways. The most obvious is the introduction of or direct reference to the material in each successive movement; thus the effect is cumulative because by the time the last movement has been reached there are references to everything which has preceded it. The principal theme of the first movement is often quoted *in extenso* as a climax. Each movement has its own particular themes and the work continually gathers itself about itself, so to speak, snowball fashion. Another method is to base the entire material of each movement on the initial phrase or phrases. In this case everything becomes a permutation of something already heard. The germ may be a short theme of no great musical significance, in fact, the less significant it is, the more opportunities it presents. The work, therefore, grows out of itself. Sometimes the basis may be a mere succession of notes which arise out of the progress of the work. These notes not being sounded thematically at any time, become apparent as the work progresses. A more abstruse way is to use mere fragments of separate melodies in the make-up of the successive subjects. This often calls for a good deal of imagination on the part of the listener and takes a great deal for granted.

The use of a motto theme can have a disastrous effect upon the reaction of the listener, for the ear is always conscious of what is happening. The process becomes analytical instead of emotional. This, of course, is only the case when the 'motto' is a distinct theme, as in Vincent d'Indy's Symphony in B flat which grows a mountain out of the smallest type of molehill. When the 'motto' is merely a note-succession, the aural process works differently and instead of being constantly aware, the ear simply becomes conscious of the connection and origin as the work proceeds, and the emotion is absorbed unselfconsciously. This Albert Roussel achieved in his Symphony in G minor; Roussel was not a direct Franck pupil but he obtained the technique of the Schola Cantorum at the hands of d'Indy, using just what he felt peculiar to his individuality and leaving the rest alone.

The advantage of the system is, as has been stated, that the work is one organic whole and the movements cannot be separated. This is perfectly logical if one is prepared to consider a symphony or sonata in several movements as one continuous work, with breaks, as it were. Those who look for conflict of ideas and emotions find it lacking in contrast, and certainly in the hands of an inexperienced composer it does tend to mono-tony; it serves also to emphasise the architecture, and the means tend to become the end. D'Indy himself always set his face against this danger. 'All processes are good provided they are but the means to the end, and not the end in themselves.'

It lessens the necessity for extended development of themes and use of the imagination. Invention takes the place of inspira-tion; hence it can be a short cut. *Grove* (Fuller-Maitland Edi-tion) suggests that Liszt used the metamorphosis of themes simply because he was so busy in other directions that it saved a lot of thought and trouble. This theory (with which the author does not agree) if not exactly complimentary to Liszt's powers of inspiration, says a lot for his genius as an architect.

The whole thing, whether or not the cyclic form is the ideal one for its purpose, depends entirely on the point of view of the individual, and it is impossible to state categorically the right or wrong of the matter.

It is often denied that Franck invented the cyclic form. D'Indy mentions a work called 'Sonata' published by Liszt in 1837 which is built entirely upon one theme. This so-called 'Sonata' is in one movement only and is more of a 'Fantaisie dramatique' than a real sonata. Both M de Bréville and M Ropartz are of the opinion that it cannot be considered the parent of Franck's idea. Further, M Julien Tiersot sees the cyclic idea in an extremely youthful *Deuxième Sonate*, the last unac-knowledged work before the 'official' Op. 1, namely, the first Trios. Franck was then a boy and knew nothing of Liszt. M Ropartz suggests that Franck, even at that early age, 'took as his point of departure certain works of Beethoven with which he was fundamentally acquainted and he created his own form from deductions obtained from the great Beethoven variation. I see in the extreme youth of the composer no valid objection to this opinion. During the course of his career he gave many proofs of genius. In any case, there is no influence of either Leborne or Reicha in this connection.'

Were it not for that early *Deuxième Sonate* we might be bound to regard the inception of the idea as emanating from Liszt; but Franck gave Liszt his early cyclic Trio in 1842. Liszt began the composition of *Les Préludes*, the first of the symphonic poems, in 1845. Franck composed *Ce qu'on entend sur la montagne* about this time. Although he cannot be said to have actually invented the use of accumulated material (since traces of it can be found in earlier composers) he did at least turn it into a living force and establish it. M de Bréville tells us that never did he impose or even recommend the use of the cyclic form to his pupils. He left it to them. The fact that they used it was entirely an act of their own volition.

It is worth while considering this form at some length, to find out how it became such a pillar of Franckian influence. M de Bréville says that it was 'd'Indy who, seeing the possibilities of the process, analysed and developed it in his treatise on composition'.

In his enthusiasm d'Indy finds precedents which may have been coincidence, but, in his view, are sufficient authority to claim that the cyclic form is used in some of Beethoven's works. This magnification of fragmentary and momentary references strains things a little, but it is worth while discussing the evidence.

The fact that Beethoven introduced a few bars of the Scherzo into the finale of the Fifth Symphony and the themes of the Ninth Symphony in its finale does not really entitle us to consider the works as 'cyclic', although it is an obvious way of binding everything together. Franck does this in the finale of the string quartet. D'Indy also quotes at some length from the 'Pastoral' Symphony, finding direct relationship between certain short figures. As so many of the themes in this Symphony consist of notes of the common chord, the resemblance can hardly be avoided. It is analogous, to a certain extent, with the Wagnerian leitmotiv. If every time a composer makes reference to previous material during the course of a movement we are invited to consider its whole form 'cyclic', every work ever written must be cyclic, which is absurd. It is only when reference appears constantly and consistently throughout that we can feel safe in so describing it.

55

Of all the Beethoven symphonies, it is the sixth which has this interdependence of movements, solely because of its subject and character. It is for the reader to decide for himself whether or not the examples quoted by d'Indy in his *Cours de Composition musicale* Vol. II are intentional or accidental.

Ex. 5

D'Indy also quotes some of the piano sonatas as further evidence, particularly the *Pathétique* in which he sees cyclic proof in the following little figure which emerges as a definite theme in the first and third movements, but is merely a link in the second.

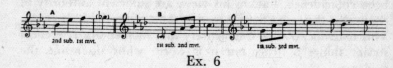

Ex. 6

More convincing, perhaps, is the reference to the A flat sonata Op. 110 in which the principal theme of the first movement does bear a kind of relationship to the fugue subject.

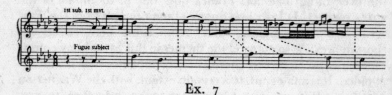

Ex. 7

D'Indy is, however, quite convincing when he quotes a Suite-Sonata by Giovanni Battista Vitali (1644-1692). Here it is undeniable that the whole work is derived from the germ of the first movement.

Ex. 8

This complete use of the cyclic form is admitted by d'Indy as not occurring again until Franck's violin sonata, the method suggested as used by Beethoven being fragmentary.

The more one continues, the more one becomes capable of seeing something in everything. It may be often far-fetched, but Vincent d'Indy was no mere dilettante or dull-minded professor. He was a composer of importance in the history of music and an exceedingly cultured man. His opinions, therefore, cannot be turned down or ignored without the fullest consideration and sympathy.

The strongest point against the form is that it tends to monotony and inevitability. Thus, in a symphony like that by Chausson, which follows its model very closely, the working-out is obvious all the time—but Franck was a genius and Chausson was not. Nevertheless, it makes the following of the work easy and logical to those who listen in this way. Vincent d'Indy in his enormous Symphony in B flat carries the process to its fullest extent. The work is built upon two germs of little thematic note, yet d'Indy contrives to give them the supremely important place in the whole Symphony. The fact that he described the work as the conflict between good and evil need not blind us to the musical logic of the climactic chorale, where the theme of evil is (rightly) in the bass o'ertopped by that of good. The germs, however, are definite themes and not note-succession. This latter process is found in the Third Symphony of Albert Roussel. The result is satisfactory in every respect because the music just 'happens'.

The difference between Franck and d'Indy is that with the former it is the emotion which plays a higher part than the construction, and the thought is directed by the process. With the latter we are not as conscious of the music as we are of the construction. Ravel said of the disciples of d'Indy that they would not allow emotion. Franck was a great creative genius; d'Indy was a great musician who was also an architect. This comparison between master and pupil is important because during their lives the latter was very much wider known than the former, and his works are the natural expansion of his master's theories.

Franck, his pupils, and Liszt were not, of course, the only composers to use the system. Brahms does so in his first two piano sonatas and in the third movement of the Second Symphony. Nevertheless, the form is the hall-mark of the Franck tradition and carries with it certain principles which cannot be gainsaid. The greatest of these is clarity in all its aspects.

There is, however, another form in which he excelled and whose constituent elements are not far removed from the essence of the cyclic form. This is the variation upon a theme. There is probably no form which is more conducive to dullness and 'correct' writing. It is extremely easy to point to visual derivations which, aurally, carry no weight. It was said many years ago, apropos Strauss's *Ein Heldenleben*, that one could combine a hundred melodies provided one did not mind what they sounded like. Conversely, one can vary a theme in any way one likes provided that the cohesion is maintained; thus it may be a virtue to be able to combine a theme in its original form with an inverted and/or retrogressive version provided that the combination is aurally satisfactory. A story, which lacks verification, tells of Vincent d'Indy. A student showed him some music in which everything was in double and triple counterpoint and combinations of themes, the whole sounding like nothing on earth. D'Indy asked him what it was and received the answer that it was 'visual counterpoint'. Staggered for the moment by this explanation, d'Indy went over to a picture and invited the student to listen to it, saying that it was an 'aural painting'. Then followed an explosion of wrath which, coming from the lips of so dignified a man, astonished those who heard it. It is very easy to invert a theme in augmentation, combining it with a version in diminution, duly decorated and ornamented, but if the musical or æsthetic effect is merely one of erudition and not of emotion (in the best sense of the word) then it is pointless. In other words, to quote d'Indy again, all processes are good, provided that they are the means to the end and not the end in themselves.

Franck's mastery of variation is apparent in every work he wrote, whether the evidence be in the variation of a short phrase or of the whole material. This is one of the reasons for maintaining that the heritage of Bach and Beethoven descended on him, but there is no implication that his music is as great as theirs. Whether it was the building up from a rhythmic germ, as in the *Variations symphoniques*, the creation of an entire work upon its own material, as the *Prélude, Aria, et Finale*, or the complete variation, as in the first Choral and the use of the Passacaglia form in the second, the direct descent from Beethoven is obvious. The arabeske of Bach we find in the infinite melody of the third Choral and the *Prélude, Choral et Fugue*, an arabeske which is not so decorative, but is just as rhapsodic.

He inherited the high æsthetic ideals and the fervent sincerity of the two great composers. The greatness of Bach and Beethoven largely lies in their infinite variety. Franck was limited in range of expression and in technique. There is too distinct a kinship between one work and another and the letter is too much a uniform pattern. There was no French tradition for Franck to work upon. Instead, he had to formulate it himself in the large forms. This he did and it is significant that after the early Trios he put aside all German influence—an examination of *Ce qu'on entend sur la montagne* shows that this work marked the dividing line between the two cultures and may very well have been the reason why Franck did not allow it to be published.

His fugue subjects cannot in any way be compared with those of Bach and for the reason that they are very Gallic in nature. Bach used the form to express the deepest emotions he felt. Franck used it only incidentally.

Dramatically he was not at home. His operas have negative qualities which in their time were positive ; but the works date like all those of their period. They lack strength and forcefulness and another Franck seems to have written them. He was incapable of writing good 'theatre'. The subjects are suitable enough and the libretti no worse than most others. The vocal writing is impeccable. When delineating anything evil he was quite out of his depth—not that his ineffable goodness made him blind to the subject, but his technique was not of that nature.

Such are the general characteristics of Franck's music. It now remains to consider the works in detail.

1845

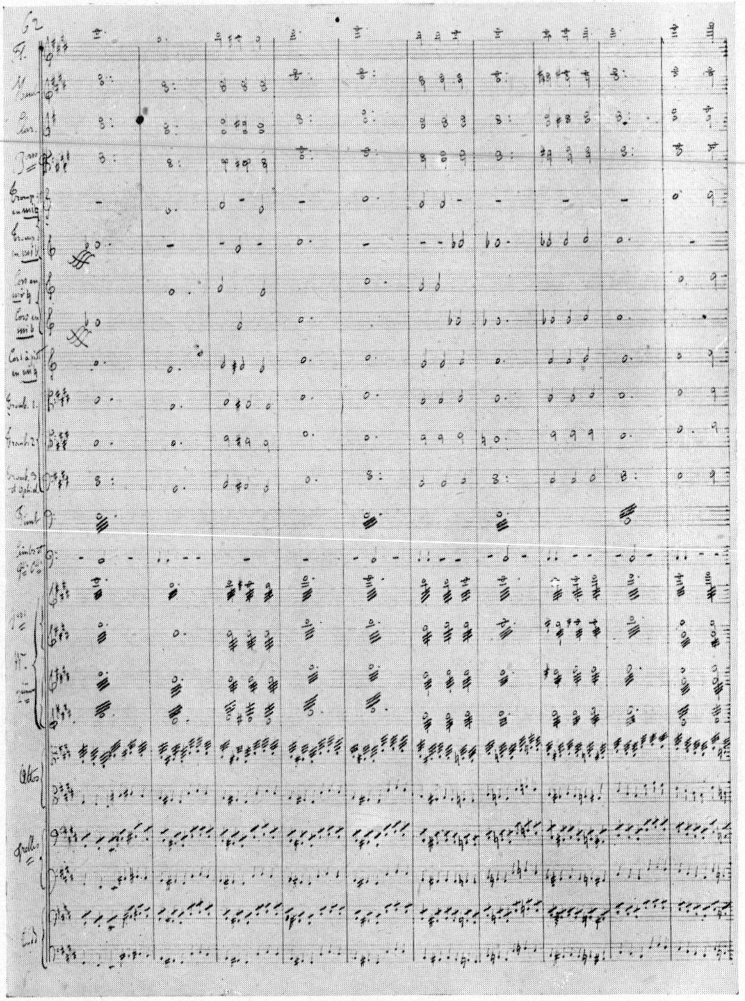

‘Ce qu’on entend sur la montagne’

Chapter Five

The Orchestral Works

THE boyish orchestral effusions can only be mentioned briefly here. They include a Piano Concerto which attempts to capture a certain grand manner and very nearly succeeds, in its limited scope. The most interesting thing about these eleven and twelve year old works is that the orchestral touch is so sure. There is no fumbling about with clefs or any of the usual mistakes so common with youth when it sets out on its first instrumental ventures. The orchestral forces are modest. His Op. 4, written at the age of eleven and a half, demands flutes, oboes, bassoons, horns and strings—*Variations Brillantes sur un original Thême*. The similar *Variations Brillantes* (always!), *sur La Ronde Favorite de Gustave III* add clarinets; the composer was then twelve and it was his Op. 8. The *Grand Concerto en Si mineur* Op. 11, however, is more ambitious and calls for trumpets, three trombones and percussion. It need hardly be said that none of these works could possibly be played today, even in a concert of historical or curious music.

The early Symphony was not available at the Bibliothèque Nationale in August 1947, but M Julien Tiersot says that its orchestration was for ordinary full orchestra which, as has been stated, played 'all out' nearly all the time.

It is when we get to *Ce qu'on entend sur la montagne* that real interest begins. Victor Hugo's poem deals with the struggle between good and evil, the voices heard on the mountain being those of Nature and Humanity. The poet climbs the mountain and there he hears:

un bruit large, immense, confus,
Plus vague que le vent dans les arbres touffes…

The sounds become confused and disguised,

Deux voix dans cette voix l'une à l'autre mêlées…
L'une venait des mers; chant de gloire! hymne heureux…
L'autre qui s'élevait de la terre où nous sommes,
Etait triste: c'était le murmure des hommes.

On the one side there is the ocean, on the other, the earth and mankind. At the end the poet mixes in his dream the song of nature with the cry of the human race.

The music is definite impressionism at the opening. A gently moving viola theme under sustained violin harmonics sets an atmosphere of mystery which anticipates Debussy. Eventually a clear chordal theme appears which interests us because it is one of the first instances of melodic derivation of one theme from another:

Ex. 9

'A' becomes as follows a little later, and 'B' in Ex. 13 is similarly derived.

Ex. 10

There is no doubt as to the composer of the next progression,

Ex. 11

nor is there very much with this bass passage (note the augmented fourth).

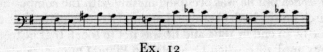

Ex. 12

Up to this point the thought and expression has been Gallic but with the next theme it becomes Teutonic, especially when it is thundered out in G major *fff* through triplet reiterations in what we should now call the Liszt style. Observe its derivation at 'B' from Ex. 9.

Ex. 13

The anticipation of Liszt's *Les Préludes* is quite astonishing. Another theme is prophetic in its contours.

Ex. 14

It is interesting to see how Franck even at this early stage in his career uses the change from minor to major mode, a feature which became an integral part of his technique in his maturity.

This work could take its place in an *historical* concert with profit. As music, of course, it is but the shadow of what was to come and with its uncertain and alternating Gallic and Teutonic influences is vague and indefinite. However, it is a real historical document and the longer one reads the neatly written MS the more one is convinced that Liszt must have known it. There are few early works by any composer which are so prophetic and so interesting.

After *Ce qu'on entend sur la montagne* Franck wrote no purely orchestral work until 1876. During that period he wrote *Rédemption* but he was occupied mainly with the composition of church music, both choral and organ. His early piano music had come to an end in 1865 and he was not to touch that instrument again until 1879 when he wrote the Piano Quintet. Abstention from a genre, therefore, seems to have been one of his characteristics. When he returned to the orchestra he was more experienced and had not only heard much orchestral music but had read the scores of his contemporaries as they became available.

Les Éolides is based upon a poem by Leconte de Lisle which, in these matter-of-fact days, is full of extravagant romanticism. The poem is addressed to the breezes who were the daughters of Æolus, and it describes their flight over deserts from sunny lands. The general spirit is fanciful—'Capricious kisses', 'Return again, breezes of the divine months; And, as ye pass, pour from your golden urns to us below, love, grace, harmony' are two typical quotations. Franck took endless trouble over this work, and regarded the poem very literally. On the rough sketches there is the pencil note 'Développement capricieux', so we know what the middle section was about. The advantage of listening to a work which is more general in atmosphere than direct in narration is that we are not constantly worrying as to where we have got in the story, and what any passage is representing.

If we think of the best known symphonic poems, we find them to be mostly dramatic and noisy—*Don Juan, Ein Heldenleben, Romeo and Juliet, Thamar, Les Préludes*; taken at random, each one illustrates the point. It is only when we reach Debussy that the symphonic poem becomes changed with *L'Après-Midi* and quietness. A reasonably peaceful work of this nature, therefore, is welcome. At the other end of the scale there are the facile symphonic poems of Saint-Saëns, admirable in portraiture and commonplace in material. It may be that the idea of the symphonic poem as an intensely dramatic and masterful work was the reason that *Les Éolides* was not performed in this country until 29th August 1914, when it received its baptism under Sir Henry Wood at a Prom. Indeed, the critic of the *Musical Times* referred to its 'refined beauty and strength' seemingly as something quite unexpected.

Les Éolides is beautiful as well as interesting. It is one of the earliest instances of Franck chromaticism and semitonal mobility. The music slides along with the utmost polish and gentleness and there is complete continuity throughout. Reference has already been made to the rough pencil sketches which exist, showing how Franck worked at the main theme. Some see the shadow of *Tristan* across it, but it is doubtful if Franck knew this work at the time. In any case the idiom became so intensely personal to him that any charges of either plagiarism or 'being under the influence of' can be refuted on this ground.

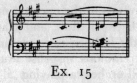

Ex. 15

The whole work is tinged with this veiled semitonality. There is constant movement onwards and onwards—indeed, the music seems to stop only by general consent of the players. The effect at the end is to want another movement; it hardly sounds complete in itself. Only once did Franck reach this consistency of movement in a work of similar texture, and that was in *Psyché*, written in 1887 and described as a 'Symphonic Poem for Chorus and Orchestra'.

The breezes with which this work is concerned are truly feathery and gentle. They get under way after some seventy-eight bars of introductory matter which deals entirely with the figure quoted in Ex. 15. It is at this point that it is extended and the melodic line acquires curve and poise:

Ex. 16

Of canonic writing there is a profusion.

The wood-wind reiterated chords pointed by harp touches give the lightness. The cyclic idea appears to be pronounced at this point—'appears' is used advisedly because the use of the fragment of Ex. 15 in diminution as an accompaniment may be fortuitous and thought far-fetched. Particularly warm is the doubling of the theme in the clarinets and later in the first violins and cellos two octaves apart, a device used frequently by later French composers. The theme, therefore, is each side of the staccato accompaniment. Admirers of Ravel will remember that he often did this.

Franck asks for a high dynamic, treble forte, at the climax. Ere long there is a return to the opening material in charming canonic treatment between flute and clarinet. He uses that wonderful effect of the full orchestra playing pianissimo which gives a feeling of tremulous suspense and is infinitely more exciting than the full orchestra playing 'all out', if, perhaps, a different kind of excitement. The work ends very quietly.

The orchestra is quite small—double wood wind, two horns cornet à pistons, trumpet, percussion, harp and strings. With this modest force he attains the maximum of effect. It is all perfectly charming. There is none of the classical Franck to be seen except, perhaps, in the frequent use of canonic imitation which in itself is no criterion of classical outlook. It is the music which heralded Debussy and impressionism, but unlike the impressionist music it is all perfectly clear and nowhere are there obscurity of detail, mists or fogs. Its popularity in France, achieved only after some struggle and a considerable lapse of time, is perfectly understandable.

Franck's next essay in orchestral music was not written until 1882 and was a very different matter. Once more he worked on a literary basis. This was the period of the macabre, when anything at all spooky or savouring of the romanticism of evil was seized upon by poets, painters, and musicians. Franck fell a victim to a ballade by Bürger—with what result can be imagined. Berlioz or Liszt would have run riot on it and made it a mountain of horrific and ominous music. Unfortunately, so to speak, Franck could not forget to be musical and musicianly. His musical picture of the Ballade is too naïve to convince us, yet the whole work admirably draws the succeeding events.

Briefly, it tells the story of a huntsman who refused to attend the summons of the bell calling him to St Hubert's Mass and rode straight through the assembling worshippers. For this crime he was condemned to perpetual hunting, a kind of 'Wandering Jew', or landborne 'Flying Dutchman' with an affinity to our Herne the Hunter'. It is easy to ridicule such a subject in these prosaic days, but to reduce it to the level of being about 'a wicked hunter who would not go to church', as has been done, is about as sensible as describing *Tristan und Isolde* as being about 'two lovers who could not get married, so they took poison'. Nevertheless, here is the literal translation of the extract from the Ballade, and I can only assure the reader that nothing has been altered in any way to make the story more or less horrific or moral.

It was on Sunday morning. In the distance were heard the joyful sound of bells and the religious hymns of the crowd. Sacrilege! The fierce Count of the Rhine has blown his hunting horn!
'Tally-ho! Tally-ho!'
The hunt rushes through the corn, the moors and the meadows—
'Stop, Count, I pray you—listen to the pious hymn.'
'No. Tally-ho! Tally-ho!'
'Stop, listen, I implore you, take care...'
'No', and the cavalcade hurries on like a hurricane.
Suddenly the Count is alone, his horse refuses to go further. He blows his hunting horn but there is no sound.... A dismal, pitiless voice curses him.
'Sacrilege', it says, 'Be thou for ever hunted by Hell.'
Then flames spurt out from every direction. The Count mad with terror, flies away always faster and faster, pursued by demons, at day through abysses, at night through the air.

This perfect nonsense is typical of its period but no doubt future generations will have many a laugh at our expense. However, the point with which we are concerned is that Franck underlined the story very literally and clearly. Nothing is left to the imagination. He probably enjoyed himself hugely while writing it.

Le Chasseur maudit is a long work but concise and well-balanced. It is extremely easy to follow through its literary progress. Presumably it might be considered as a 'good introduction to the symphonic poem' for those beginning the adventure of music, but it is not the music of a child.

It opens with an unmistakable hunting-horn call:

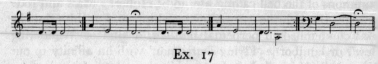

Ex. 17

Under the pealing bell, this theme takes on a quasi-religious garb and clearly indicates the playing of an organ. Through this theme, which has considerable dignity, more hunting horns are heard:

Ex. 18

The huntsman, however, ignores the summons to church and 'the hunt is up':

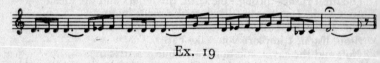

Ex. 19

The galloping hooves of the horses are clearly marked and the chase is a hot one, the theme of Ex. 19 becoming the theme of the actual chase. It is extremely noisy and rhythmic and its progress is held up while the curse is delivered with bell, book, and candle. The accursed huntsman now cannot stop, and off he goes at top-speed to his perpetual doom. The music piles itself up from rhythmic compound triple time to simple duple, and with a headlong rush it dies to a treble piano drum roll, to end with a loud chord on the full orchestra.

The orchestration fails in two ways only. In the first place Franck relies on the cellos for more than the usual number can give, and the church theme is often drowned by the weight of the wind above it. In the second place, the bass part is not mobile enough in those places where mobility would seem to be needed. Otherwise the scoring is masterly and rich. Four bassoons are used, thus obtaining quasi-horn chords while the actual horns are engaged with thematic matters. Two cornets à pistons are included, and these add brilliance which must be heard to be believed. A particularly nice effect is the writing for flutes and bassoon, the former in their low register, while the strings soar up on a gentle theme:

Ex. 20

The curse, of course, is not that of *The Ring* but it is no less effective within its small compass.

There is no subtlety and the whole work has a stamp of naïveté about it, but it is great fun and extremely effective. It is still played when other works on similar subjects have been forgotten. It came at the time when romanticism was approaching its full expression. It says more than any of the Saint-Saëns symphonic poems, and, as a symphonic poem, is worthy of more serious consideration than the *Danse Macabre* (even though this harmless work was hissed at its first performance) or any others of the set by its prolific composer. It has not the power of evil delineation shown in Berlioz's *Witches' Sabbath* or Meyerbeer's 'brisk ballet of perjured nuns', as Dr Percy Scholes terms this section of *Robert le Diable*, or in Liszt's *Mephisto* waltz. The opposite number of these works is found in the Victorian melodramas with their trapdoors and fire-spitting demons dragging the villain's lost soul to their lair. *Le Chasseur maudit* may be too respectable but it is never cheap or commonplace.

Two years later Franck composed his third symphonic poem, making a return to the piano. For the subject he took Victor Hugo's poem from *Les Orientales*—'Les Djinns'—the Arabian spirits which are able to change themselves into elements of good or evil. The poem describes their flight over a city and Victor Hugo lays it out in one continuous stanza in the form of a lozenge. Beginning with one word he adds another to each line until the maximum of ten is reached ; he then reverses the process. This is impossible to reproduce in music, of course, but the poem itself shows the appearance and disappearance of the spirits very graphically.

Like all good composers Franck studied the works of his contemporaries as well as those of the great masters. His own technique had broadened and he devised a pianism to fit it. His early virtuosic works stood him in good stead because he was able to use their technique allied to a new musical content, without any thought to the technical display which had necessarily occupied him in the days of his youth. It must be remembered when considering music of any highly stylized period that what are now conventions were at that time novelties. Today we fight as shy of the chord of the diminished seventh as possible; at that time it was a chord of the highest value and the period might well be regarded as seeing it at the climax of its career. Henceforth it was to be avoided.

There is, therefore, a considerable amount of pianism of the Liszt nature in *Les Djinns*, but never deliberately virtuosic as Liszt would have viewed it. If arpeggio accompaniment to a melody had become a convention, Franck eased the convention by the way he spread the notes. They are by no means impossible of execution; they merely require a wider spread of the hands, and whereas any other composer might have been content to make the left hand perfunctory and to take little trouble or thought over the mere padding, Franck obviously regarded it as of equal importance with the melody. Thus we have awkwardness like this:

Ex. 21

Les Djinns is *of* the grand manner but not quite *in* it. There is a good deal of passage work, the hands playing boldly in double octaves, and some rather ordinary arpeggio figures which keep the pianist conveniently busy and the music reasonably moving. There are no cadenzas as such, but the progress of the music is held up by this kind of thing:

Ex. 22

which has been the prop of so many succeeding composers.

Les Djinns is not very graphic. The result is that the listener tends to forget its literary basis and hears it as a concert piece for piano and orchestra in one movement. Franck uses his favourite key of F sharp, but the music is not in it for very long and speedily commences on a tour of most of the other sharp keys. No one could call it pretentious. It says its say quite straightforwardly, and that is one thing, at any rate, for which we can be thankful in a work for piano and orchestra. Pianists enjoy playing it.

Historically it is of the utmost importance if we consider that piano concertos by French composers were almost non-existent at the time, the only real competitor with Franck in the genre being Saint-Saëns. Franck's pupils, Vincent d'Indy and Alexis de Castillon followed in their master's footsteps. *Les Djinns* has even more significance in the Franck canon as it prepared the ground for the two big works for piano solo and, more especially, for the *Variations symphoniques* for piano and orchestra.

The writer hopes he has shown that his love is not blind, at any rate where Franck is concerned; but when we regard these variations, then he is absolutely certain that we have a flawless work and as near perfection as human composer can hope to get in a work of this nature.

Composed in 1885 when Franck was in the full flood of his creative inspiration, it is amongst the happiest music ever written and therefore amongst the most moving. The genius of Franck was well suited to the variation form as will be seen in the chapter on the organ *Chorals*, and he was able to infuse it with a musical element which is often absent from what is basically something cerebral. We shall consider the *Variations symphoniques* in complete detail not only because it is one of Franck's best works but because it was music unheard of at its period and still stands unique today.

The piano concerto as a genre had become established in the nature of a work for a soloist with orchestral accompaniment. Even the best examples of Mozart and Beethoven kept an eye upon the element of technique, although both composers placed the music *per se* as of paramount importance. The 'grand manner' had begun to penetrate with Liszt. The Franck-period concertos were those of Schumann, Mendelssohn and Brahms. The solitary Schumann example placed the onus on the piano but kept the traditional orchestral tuttis well to the fore, and although the orchestral writing in the first movement is often perfunctory and in the other two movements at times seems almost in the way, it is of some importance in the general ensemble and suggests an attempt to return to the 'concertante' idea, in which soloist and orchestra are equal. The Mendelssohn concertos obeyed the laws of tradition and the emphasis was placed on the soloist. Brahms combined the two elements in his D minor and B flat concertos, with the result that the former was well and truly hissed at its first performance. He added a considerable amount of the 'grand manner', but this lay only in the general conception. The ideas were big and the music correspondingly broad. He, like Schumann, kept the technique within the scope of the thematic material. Liszt was interested solely in the piano part, which he wrote for himself. The orchestra, therefore, was frequently relegated to a subordinate position and in the tuttis devoted almost entirely to repetition of the principal themes. The tradition of the cadenza was handed from Liszt to Tchaikovsky and the latter was the last composer to use it in all its glory—but these cadenza passages are more thematic than mere pianistic display, and although the player has to show off his prowess in order to play the notes, this display is not the end in itself.

Ravel complained that the piano concerto was too often a battle between piano and orchestra, and cited the concertos of

Mozart and Saint-Saëns as ideals. The former he held up as a model of content and the latter as a model of clarity. Both these elements he would have found in Franck's *Variations symphoniques*, but he was naturally prejudiced against anything connected, however remotely, with the Schola Cantorum. The descent of Franck in this respect is from Mozart and Schumann. From the former he got slenderness of means and grace of expression; from the latter, clarity combined with a degree of breadth, and the general 'concertante' idea. Although Schumann had indeed this latter principle in mind, he was unable to carry it out convincingly. He lacked just what Franck had by nature, a scholarly mind which was able to direct but not control his inspiration. Franck placed the piano in the middle of the orchestra and wove round it the tissues of orchestral colour, making it part and parcel of the ensemble. The *Variations symphoniques*, therefore, are all of a piece.

The balance is perfect throughout and the orchestra required consists only of double wood wind, four horns, two trumpets, kettledrums, and strings. Formally, it is most interesting and novel. Franck was not concerned with writing 'variations on a theme'; his basis was that of the 'thème varié', a work built on a number of ramifications of a theme. In this way he obviated the continual stopping which the former principle involves, in which each variation is a complete entity in itself. Two themes are used of considerable contrasting nature, themes not very linear, but pithy enough to allow extension. The opening section is in simple ternary form and the fact that the work is on the lines of a thème varié does not preclude him from writing variations of some length. The closing pages of the work are in pure sonata form, with limited middle section but sufficient to make a clear break between enunciation and recapitulation. There is no other work in existence which is so completely self-contained.

The two themes are as follows:

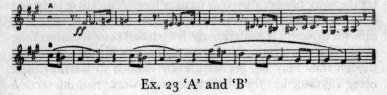

Ex. 23 'A' and 'B'

'A' is repeated, slightly varied, the initial rhythm rising instead of falling on its second appearance. 'B' follows a third higher with the slightest variant of the last complete bar.

'A' then appears in the bass, with emphatic treatment. This constitutes Variation One. Variation Two is chordal on the orchestra, the piano filling-in with simple arpeggio figures in the two hands at the end of each stanza. This section in A major is important because later it appears in F sharp and becomes another variation in itself, but more varied than simply changing the mode.

Ex. 24

This concludes the first section of the ternary form. The episode consists of a complete variation based mainly on 'B' but with reference to 'A' half way through.

Ex. 25

This is for piano alone.

We then return to the first section modified and extended, with a bold statement of 'A' followed by 'B' almost as it first appeared, but ending in C sharp major. A fragmentary version of Ex. 24 over a cello reference to 'A' leads to the third variation, and from this point we have a succession of variations. So far the work has been in clear ternary form. Vincent d'Indy sees it as an introduction to the whole work. With this view it is difficult to agree, considering the length and completeness of the piano solo variation. In any case the two themes, sectional though they may be, are too clearly defined to warrant their being anything but the whole basis of the work; had this section been introductory the themes as stated would have been merely fragments of what would follow.

The following succession of variations lead straight into one another. Ex. 24 is in F sharp minor as another piano solo, chordal and serene. The orchestra enters with a quaver version of 'A' and there is much antiphonal writing between piano and orchestra.

Ex. 26

This constitutes Variation Four.

In contrast the violas and cellos play Ex. 26 while the piano moves in smooth quaver chords in which for the first time there is real pianism—that underneath Ex. 24 is hardly enterprising enough to call for comment. A bridge passage leads to Variation Six in which the theme is disguised with real ingenuity. The spacing of the right hand conforms with Franck's own wide stretch, yet it causes no difficulty to the experienced pianist. This is based on 'A'.

Ex. 27

The strings punctuate with pizzicato chords but do not add thematically or materially to the main issue.

So far everything has been quiet and smooth, but Variation Seven plunges immediately into 'A' while the piano emphasizes

75

with chords on the second half of the beat, alternating with octave passages of no bravura qualities. The roles are interchanged, but this is not enough to constitute a variation in itself, since the variant is instrumental rather than thematic.

A new theme is heard.

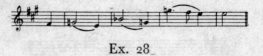

Ex. 28

Variation Eight places 'A' on the strings under a triplet piano part.

The storm dies down and after a modal cadence into the key of F sharp major, the cello plays a perfectly beautiful version of 'A' under mere pianism in two parts, the top of which suggests a hint at 'A' in another form, but this may quite probably be fortuitous.

Ex. 29

A change to the suavities of F sharp minor and under perfectly smooth, unthematic pianism and sustained string chords, the cellos play a lovely version of 'B'. They linger long and lovingly, and this tenth variation Vincent d'Indy regards as a sorrowful farewell.

The mood alters and after some semitonal semiquavers, a trill heralds the last section which, as has been said, is a movement in sonata form. Franck says good-bye to any regrets which may have appeared in the music so far, and launches into a scherzo-like movement which is architecturally perfectly proportioned and æsthetically perfectly delightful.

After a short introduction with antiphonal writing between bassoons and horns, and oboes and clarinets (which will be heard as the material of the solo part), the cellos and basses play a version of 'B'.

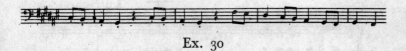

Ex. 30

The piano enters at the end of the trill (which has been continuous) with the final lay-out of the introductory bars. This is a cheerful variant of 'A' in F sharp major.

Ex. 31

It constitutes the principal subject of this small sonata movement.

A new tune comes in,

Ex. 32

to be followed by another delightfully picked out on the piano; this will be found to have a distinct affinity with the opening version of 'B'.

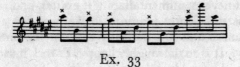

Ex. 33

The music rushes to a headlong climax, suddenly stops and the orchestra thunders out the main theme, going straight from F sharp major to D Major, the effect being electrical. The second subject follows in B flat, based on 'A'.

77

Ex. 34

The middle section deals with this and other material and the exhilaration is held up by a cleverly concealed presentation of the main theme ('B' in this case) on the piano.

Ex. 35

The recapitulation takes up the story over a cross-rhythm with the piano which usually sounds to the listener on first hearing as if something had gone wrong with the time. For the rest the music deals with the previous material, as all recapitulations should, and the work ends with a canonic coda.

Such detailed description may read rather drily, but no apology is offered because this wonderful work requires such treatment. It is wonderful because of the perfect good taste and restraint shown throughout, as well as its consummate workmanship. Æsthetically it is perfectly satisfactory. It exults, it dreams, but never sentimentalizes ; it excites, and never pontificates. It is sufficiently pianistic to warrant the attention of virtuoso pianists and it is perfectly easy for the unenlightened ear to enjoy. It is so thoroughly happy, Franck must have been on the top of the world when he was writing it.

Exception is sometimes taken to the variations for the piano alone, and to the one in which the 'cello plays such an important role, the objection being that the orchestra hangs about with nothing to do. This is more a credit than otherwise. Other composers might have been tempted to write sustaining harmonies which mean and add nothing, or niggling little entries which give an air of busyness. At these moments Franck had nothing for the orchestra to say, so refrained from saying it. In the second place, only the cello tone could give the true interpretation of his thought. As well blame a composer for an orchestral tutti which keeps the soloist hanging about. No reproach of organ influence can be made. This work is a model both æsthetically and architecturally. It signalled a point of departure from the 'grand manner'. It showed, too, that a normally serious-minded composer could reach another plane without losing dignity. There are few works which are so equal.

Its greatest descendant is Vincent d'Indy's *Symphonie cévenole* which is described as being for 'orchestra and piano'. Other composers who have used the basic principle but have not succeeded in reaching this great height are, notably, Boëllmann in his *Variations symphoniques* for cello and orchestra and, later, Dohnányi in his *Variations on a Nursery Song*, the latter being intentionally a light-hearted work. The point of contact lies in the fact that virtuoso players need not hesitate to play any of them. Virtuosity is needed, but it is hidden thematically.

Vincent d'Indy describes the years 1884 to 1889 as remarkable for a return to pure symphonic form on the part of certain French composers. The three concerned were Lalo, Saint-Saëns, and Franck. The first composed a thoroughly delightful and characteristic Symphony in G minor, of imaginative and fascinating qualities. The second, who was by that time established as within the canon of French art, composed his Symphony in C minor, sometimes known as the *Symphonie avec orgue* because that instrument plays a background role in the score—as does the piano. The Saint-Saëns symphony is as solemn as that by Lalo is gay; the *Dies irae* plays a prominent part and does not help materially towards happiness. It was performed in England in 1885 and did not appear in France until 1887. Franck's symphony was commenced in 1886, finished in 1888 and performed the following year. By the time Saint-Saëns's was played in Paris, Franck's was well in the process of composition.

These three symphonies have but one survivor, that by Franck. Lalo's has gone into absolutely undeserved neglect and in this country few seem to know that it exists. Saint-Saëns's has also passed into comparative oblivion from which it appears now and again, though rarely again. The truth is that it has no staying power or any force to make it compelling. The reason for the neglect of Lalo's is inexplicable.[1]

French music, therefore, was ready for the symphony, but Parisian audiences were not ready for a work of the nature of Franck in D minor.

Franck, as will be seen, laboured for some years in its composition, not necessarily because ideas came slowly, but because he simply had no time to devote to it. The work, however, was one which Franck was bound to write because all his strength was flowing in that direction, and it was a logical conclusion that sooner or later a symphony would be written by him.

His score contains a cor anglais and bass clarinet in addition to the ordinary wood wind, and two cornets à pistons to the brass, but only one trumpet. It was the cor anglais which caused the pother, its appearance in a symphony being something quite new within the memory of the time. However, no one seems to have objected to the bass clarinet which is also not a usual inclusion. The cornet à pistons is an instrument much advocated by Berlioz and used by nearly all French composers of the period. We avoid it in this country.

The symphony is cyclic and throughout its course various references (both in part and in extenso) to the main themes are made. The opening theme is interesting because other composers have used it.

Ex. 36

Liszt opens *Les Préludes* with it, Wagner uses it in *Die Walküre*, and, most extraordinary of all, Scriabin in the *Poème de l'Extase*. It is answered by a reposeful string theme of complete serenity.

[1] Since this was written Lalo's symphony was performed twice by the B.B.C. in 1947.

Ex. 37

The movement proper is in the nature of a 'double' and Guy Ropartz is emphatic that this is what Franck intended and how he wished it to be played. The slow opening returns, this time in F minor. A swaying syncopated figure in the bassoons gives the music momentum, and gives also the clue to a characteristic of most of the themes in the work.

Ex. 38

The movement proper then commences, again as a 'double' and also in F minor. There is considerable drive and Franck exercises his usual centralization of a note in the themes which gives poise although it holds up the movement slightly. The second subject illustrates this very suitably and it is announced on the full orchestra in a shout of triumph.

Ex. 39

The development section is long and complete and deals with a kind of discussion between the two main themes. The return of the first section (or recapitulation section) is in the pace of the original opening, no slower and no faster.

This movement is very satisfying. It is boisterous but not vulgar. The Franck chromaticism perhaps becomes a little monotonous and in some places is distinctly sentimental. The moods are well contrasted and the general spirit is sincerity and an unbounding optimism.

The second movement, marked 'allegretto', is one of the loveliest in music. It has a fine shapely tune on the cor anglais which has become much abused over the course of years.

Ex. 40

Guy Ropartz described this as 'the motive of Faith' and the name has stuck to it, although in *Grove* Harvey Grace erroneously applies it to the second subject of the first movement. The result of this description has been to formulate the theory that it is something inordinately holy. This matter will be discussed in the chapter on Franck as a man.

This tune does not make any appearance in the first movement and cannot be connected with any part of it. An episode bears a slight relation to the second subject of the first movement. After a return to the principal subject a completely different mood is introduced, led into by some discursive music between strings and wood-wind. The next episode deserves its description as 'heavenly'. It is exceedingly happy when played up to speed.

Ex. 41

The section from this point is repeated and the movement finishes with an extended coda. The form is difficult to define, but it is all perfectly clear to follow. It is the music of a happy man.

The third movement opens emphatically with a six bar introduction. The principal subject is very rhythmic and swings along in a manner very dissimilar to the other movements.

Ex. 42

The second subject is a chorale-like tune. There is no crescendo-and-back-again, and the marking is 'dolce cantabile', but it is usually given a sickening 'molto espress' effect.

See Ex. 46

After the music has re-captured the opening carefree spirit, the theme of the second subject comes in with a triplet accompaniment.

One of the most glorious climaxes in music is reached when the second subject is thundered out on the full orchestra after a strenuous passage which takes us straight to the issue, unfalteringly. Finally, even this triumph is overshadowed by the magnificence of a fortissimo statement of the second movement theme.

The symphony ends with a cyclic coda which reminds us of the first movement and both its themes, closing with the main theme of the finale.

In relation to other symphonies, this one by Franck stands by itself, although it has had some copyists. It does not satisfy the analytical mind as much as one of Brahms because it is not so complex and not so academic, in the best sense of the word. Much of it is a clear statement of themes completely unadorned and unhidden. Æsthetically, it satisfies completely, but only if performed properly. The dividing line between sentiment and sentimentalism is almost non-existent under these circumstances. Its seriousness is of a quality different from that of the Teutonic composers. It is *not* spiritual. It is the music of one who believed and whose faith was strong; but it is not a sentimental or sniveling faith. It is a faith which stood unshaken and which typified everything which was different from the French life of the period. Yet it is not religious music save that the impulse behind it is a religious expression of confidence in the ultimate future and a philosophy which overcame the disappointments of the present. The music of resignation is often insipid and simple. This music is strong but not muscular. Its happiness is not the happiness of Schubert's C major symphony or the bluffness of Beethoven's fourth, nor is it the melancholy joy of Mozart's G minor. It is akin to much of Bach and his robust profession of faith; but it is the faith of a Roman Catholic who takes everything for granted and does not question. Bach's faith was foursquare. He was also unquestioning but at the same time inquiring. Whatever doubts he may have had were set at rest by research, so to speak. Bach worshipped God as an individual. Franck worshipped Him in the mystery of the Mass, but both undoubtedly stood up and faced Him boldly when the moment arrived.

Franck's symphony is of the type which helped to establish the genre as the means whereby composers expressed their deepest and greatest thoughts. It is not an epic in any way and therein it differs from some of Beethoven's and Brahms's first and third. It is more akin to his fourth.

If the Symphony is to be judged by constructional musical standards one may say that never was there such magnificent music so badly written. It is full of pauses; its discursive moments are rarely free from interruption and argument which lead very often to nothing. There is a lot of questioning and answering. It is in clear-cut four bar phrases, in themselves a danger to continuity—in fact, it is singularly deficient in those elements which make for sustained development. No sooner does the first movement get under way than it is pulled up for the discussion of a phrase, usually in a repetitive manner, slightly varied, and invariably sequential. The climaxes are obtained too easily by means of sequence, yet the shape is exquisite. One short phrase will be repeated higher and higher, and even higher until it nearly reaches the top of the hill, and then we are often let down. When the climaxes *are* attained, the effect is tremendous, but we are conscious of a sickly, slithering chromaticism such as this:

Ex. 43

The scoring is much of a colour. Franck admitted to Pierre de Bréville that he was not a master of orchestration, yet we have *Les Éolides* as a distinct contradiction. Too often is the ear assailed by the peculiar tang of the oboe doubling the flute in unison, resembling the cornopean stop on the organ. All the time Franck seems to be extemporizing. The constant holding up of the continuity is not so much the influence of laborious stop-changing (a muscular feat in those days) as of changing from one manual to another, from Great to Swell and back again. The work would sound as well on the organ as would one of the Chorals on the orchestra.

The following extract suggests manuals and pedals:

Ex. 44

There is a lot of soloing like this:

Ex. 45

The presentation of the main subject of the second movement is one long solo on a Swell reed punctuated with chords on the

85

Choir. There is far too much indulgence in what Sir Charles Stanford called 'Full Swell Orchestration'. The next passage, sounding so appalling on trumpets, cornets and trombones, is a very different matter in terms of Swell reeds :

Ex. 46

All these points are emphasized by nearly every conductor who essays the work. It is the happy hunting ground of the 'tempo-rubato conductor' who cannot by any means be persuaded to play the music as the composer wrote it. He exaggerates everything and the work is never allowed to get a move on. It is impossible to 'interpret' this music because it speaks for itself.

The second movement is not a dirge; it is an allegretto which is analogous to certain movements in the Brahms symphonies. Yet it is usually dragged out to interminable lengths and in the middle is made to sound completely tired out. Its first appearance in the last movement necessitates a slowing up of the pace to about half if the quotation is to match up with its original announcement. The movement is made to snivel and whine like any penitent trying to be sorry for sins which he has not committed or, if he has, trying to pretend that he will not commit them again.

The two scores I have in front of me, those published by Hamelle and Eulenberg, have the direction at this point 'Les temps ont exactement le même valeur' and 'Tempo stretto come avanti'. Again, Example 46, when the whole orchestra shouts a pæan of praise, is usually drawn out and played 'molto adagio', regardless of the fact that there is no indication of any alteration. The only time when even a hint at reduction of speed can be permitted is at the final statement of the theme of the second movement, one of the most glorious and uplifting climaxes in music, when from the prevailing flat keys light is suddenly shed by a change to the sharp key of D major.

Without suggesting that the best way to perform the Symphony is to get it over as quickly as possible, it must be emphasized that its beauties and glories speak their own message. Any slowing-up is suggested by means of notes of longer value. That this distortion is of comparatively recent origin and habit is borne out by Sir Adrian Boult in a letter written to the author on 9th September 1947. In it Sir Adrian says:

I had heard the work once or twice before I had the great experience, somewhere early in the first war, of translating for Gabriel Pierné at a rehearsal with the Liverpool Philharmonic Orchestra. He also let me take his score back and copy his markings, although I found there was practically nothing of any importance that had not already been noted by the composer. He gave a very beautiful, natural, and French performance of it, quite unlike the rather exhausting Russianizing of it which was often heard in London between the wars. I note that fact because I remember having quite a long and tiresome rehearsal with the BBC Orchestra the first time I conducted it with them in 1932. They were quite unaccustomed to a natural and direct playing of the work.

Gabriel Pierné was a pupil of Franck and succeeded him at St Clothilde. His word has authority. So has that of Guy Ropartz, who gave the writer the fullest information as to how Franck himself wanted the symphony to be played.

With all these 'interpretations', the modulations, at first so striking and always well considered (and used because the musical feeling dictated them), become monotonous and inevitable by their frequency.

Probably a great deal may be laid on the literal acceptance of the term 'motif of faith'—but faith moves mountains because of its supreme joy and happiness. The shouts of joy and exaltation, the beauties of the quieter passages, the onrush of the opening of the finale, all these are not the expression of a whining ascetic. They are the unshakable faith of a believing Christian, of a man who believed in his Maker and had implicit gratitude for all the things created by Him. We are carried away on the waves of the climaxes. It is easy to sneer at the benign countenance of Franck, to bandy the word 'seraphic' about and to talk largely about 'spirituality'. One never hears sneers at the rock-like faith of Johann Sebastian Bach because his particular religion was of a less sensuous and

87

dramatic type; yet it is every bit as obvious as that of Franck.

This great work added dignity to what in France was a declining form. It was the first symphony to show the traditions of Beethoven superimposed on a Gallic mould. It opened new vistas to symphonic music. It was immediately sincere and profound. It had nothing facile about it. Its travail must have been severe but it could only have been travail with great joy. It may be technically weaker than any of the Brahms symphonies, but it is much more profound.

It has passed through the range of intense hatred to perfervid affection. Now it is fashionable to despise it.

Concurrently with the composition of the Symphony Franck worked at a symphonic poem for chorus and orchestra, *Psyché*, commencing it in 1887 and finishing it the following year. *Psyché* is a work not well known in this country, although it has been recorded.

It is in three parts, 'Psyche Asleep', 'The Gardens of Eros' and 'The Punishment—Psyche's Sufferings and Tears—Apotheosis'. The argument of the first part is as follows:

Psyche sleeps...In the dim regions of her dreams her spirit becomes aware of some perfect bliss, not of this world, which she feels will yet be hers. Suddenly the air vibrates to strange sounds... Psyche is borne away by Zephyrs to the Gardens of Eros.

The music opens with a syncopated theme over slow pulsating chords.

Ex. 47

There is nothing definite about it and a theme seems to be struggling in an endeavour to penetrate the mists. Eventually it appears.

Ex. 48

The spirit becomes charged with slight movement and we are reminded of a previous work, *Les Éolides*, one of whose themes will shortly be found at the basis of this work—not that this persuades us that there is something cyclic about the whole of Franck's output.

Ex. 49

The quiet theme of Ex. 47 is disturbed by a gentle flutter, and without a break it passes into 'Psyche borne away by the Zephyrs'. After some introductory passages an immediately recognizable theme emerges.

Ex. 50

The section is delightfully light and airy and floats along in an effortless manner, with unbroken continuity. The sections forming what might be called an 'Introduction and Allegro', in no way touch impressionism. The music is chromatic but illustrates the moods too positively.

We cannot leave this section, however, without examining the fact that it very closely resembles *Les Éolides*. The answer to this comes from M Léon Vallas who, in a letter to the author, tells how at this point Franck's inspiration 'dried up'. Apparently he kept it to himself for neither M de Bréville nor M Ropartz are able to shed any light on the problem. Henri Duparc, however, was taken into the composer's confidence, being Franck's favourite pupil, and Duparc suggested using the material of *Les Éolides* since it so admirably delineated the breezes. The quotation, therefore, may perhaps be regarded as a kind of musical footnote, as M de Bréville suggests. From our point of view the

89

result is satisfactory provided that one does not know *Les Éolides* and it is probably better that we should have this duplication which, after all, is logical, than that Franck should have 'beaten out' music on his technique rather than on his inspiration.

The argument of Part 2 ('The Gardens of Eros') is:

More beautiful than beauty's self, Psyche reclines on a bed of flowers, while rejoicing nature does homage, as to a queen. Voices murmur in her ear of the power of love...She wakes in gentle agitation...The murmuring Voices speak of the invisible spouse who is even now approaching...Enchanted, she listens and waits...In graver tones the Voices sing 'Remember! On the face of thy mystic lover thou must never look...Forget not!' The spirits are silent; but another voice is now heard, sweet yet clear; it is the voice of Eros himself. Psyche timidly answers...soon their souls commingle... All is passion, all is radiance, all is happiness...to last for ever, will Psyche but remember!

The atmosphere is charged with a certain menace, somewhat in the manner of Klingsor's Magic Garden but more anxious than evil. The music for the first time reaches a fortissimo dynamic. The themes are not very distinguished but an augmented version of Ex. 49 ties the section up with what has gone before.

The voices are heard. The music is written for sopranos, altos, and tenors, with the last-named divided into two parts for a long stretch. The second tenor could, however, be sung by baritones with consequent loss of timbre, and in these days of shortages it is better to adopt this measure than not perform the work at all.

Before considering the choral writing, the inadequacy of the English translation must be mentioned because the language itself cannot give the delicate suggestiveness of the original French. To be convincing, a great poem is necessary; the language of Keats alone is capable of conveying the complete meaning. Prosaic English sounds only absurd to our ears, and does not entirely carry along the paganism of the text and scene.

The choral writing is chaste and square. It does not attempt to elaborate or underline. One immediately thinks of the scene, indeed, of the whole work in terms of ballet. In this form it would be a delight.

The opening theme of Psyche dreams its way over a restless tremolando. The warning is delivered by the sopranos in quasi-recitative style supported by sustained chords. Eros appears.

Here follows love music of an exquisite character, slightly inflamed and thoroughly romantic but not sentimental or sickly. Two themes are paramount:

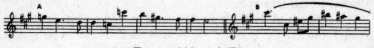

Ex. 51 'A' and 'B'

The music goes round and round with unbroken continuity, reminiscent of *Les Éolides* at a moment like this:

Ex. 52

There is no point which marks Psyche's indiscretion in asking her lover's name and it is left to the chorus which opens Part 3 to let us know that it has happened.

Psyche has disregarded the warning. 'Her punishment begins' sings the Voices—while Psyche weeps—will Eros pardon her?

Psyche weeps: her grief is measureless, for she has known measureless bliss. On earth nothing is left her but to suffer the fires of longing unappeasable—to perish in one last sad aspiration towards that ideal love which she has lost for ever, but which she still hopes to regain. 'Eros hath pardoned' sings the mysterious choir, and the universe throbs with joy... Rest now, poor Psyche! Thy yearning, strong as death, hath gone up to the great God of Love, and he himself comes down to thee: his kiss restores your former love; nature sings her old song of joy. See, in the arms of her immortal lover, Psyche soars upward from the earth, triumphant in a cloud of glory!

The chorus apostrophizes Psyche's plaint. 'See, she wanders alone by every joy forsaken.' The choral writing here is much freer than in the previous part and full use is made of canon and imitation. The choral section is followed by the orchestral picture of the wandering of Psyche, and is very beautiful and melancholy. It is built on previous themes which are easily recognizable. There is a compelling dramatic force which will be found absent from Franck's operas when we come to discuss them and which, of course, is where it should be expected. The section grows to a fevered ecstasy of triumph and Psyche is forgiven. The chorus comments upon this and the work ends on a note of high triumph.

It is difficult to write about this work in cold words. It is of all Franck's works the least full of 'Franckisms'. It rarely halts and its symphonic qualities are abundant. Sometimes we wonder why it ever stops. It does not develop but contents itself with repetition which might, but does not, pall. There are few variants of fragments such as are found in the Symphony and we are not aware of the cyclic propensities until we look for them. It is love music. It is unblushingly passionate but the passion is not of the illicit or sensual type. Sensuous it is in truth. Franck was a very human man who expressed his passion in beautiful sounds. Nowadays it is considered lacking in 'social significance' and altogether too decadent and personal to write of these things. The *élite* would have us believe that love-making is something entirely between the persons concerned and is of no concern to anyone else, nor is it of any interest whatsoever. This is as may be and the era of materialism through which we are progressing may well lead to Aldous Huxley's 'Brave New World'. In any case sensations will never alter, no matter how decadent or *démodé* they may be considered.

Franck's own attitude to the work can be found in the remark quoted by Vincent d'Indy. Whether he was ashamed of it or not one cannot say, but when *Psyché* was being discussed, Franck laid his hand on a copy of *Les Béatitudes* and said 'What I like about this work is that there is not one sensuous note in it'. This leads us to another consideration of *Psyché*.

The reader of the score may well be pardoned if he imagines that Franck took a pagan legend and treated it as such. The admirers of Franck, however, regarded him as a kind of super-human deity, one devoid of earthly passions and incapable of anything sensual.

They would have us believe, therefore, that '*Psyché* is a struggle between good and evil, between sacred and profane love'. If such had been the case, why should Franck have been so insistent upon the superiority of *Les Béatitudes*? However, the evidence must be considered.

Of the Love duet Vincent d'Indy writes as follows:

It would be difficult to regard it otherwise than as an ethereal dialogue between the soul, as the mystical author of *The Imitation of Christ* conceived it, and a seraph sent from heaven to instruct it in the eternal verities. This, at least, has been my impression of this fascinating musical picture.

Previously d'Indy had said that Franck 'aimed at making a musical paraphrase of the antique myth'.

M Derepas in a philosophical study of Franck published in 1897 makes no bones about it. Statements such as these may be extracted without damaging the context in any way.

Eros and Psyche do not express themselves in words. Their emotions are interpreted by the orchestra, and for this reason: they are not personalities. Franck, forgetful of the mythical hero and heroine, makes them the symbols of the human Soul and of Supreme Love....It is obvious that the entire work is impregnated with a breath of Christian mysticism. The sorrow of the exile on earth partakes of the accent of prayer. The exceedingly sustained harmony of the strings, the lines traced by the violins, the episodes allotted to the wind never betray the least sign of sensuous preoccupations, but only express the highest desires of a heart penetrated by the Divine Spirit.

Who said so? Franck? (But see his statement.) If so, why do not these commentators give the authority? All this seeking for divine and spiritual messages, turning nearly everything Franck wrote into a series of musical tracts, becomes very boring, and it is dangerous because it has stamped him with a completely false aura, as we shall see later on. It is this high-flown talk which has alienated Franck from so many otherwise admirers. It is ascribing something too high to a mortal with human passions.

Psyché contains some lovely sensuous music and tunes. It illustrates musically a pagan antique myth. As well describe it as a lesson to curious women as give it this bogus spiritual Christian background. It is as much a passionate love song as is The Song of Solomon, and no inner meanings or interpretations can alter either of them. Of course, it is perfectly easy to read something in everything and it is surprising that the commentators, in their eagerness for purity, have not found some kind of heavenly lesson in *Le Chasseur maudit*!

To listen to *Psyché* is a joy because it is unpretentious and straightforward. Its flow is continuous, its scoring perfectly charming in every respect. It is not great music in the sense of the Symphony, the two Piano works, or the Quartet. Its quality is refined and polished. Its eroticism is not pornographic in the way some other composers would have made it—Scriabine, for example. It is 'pure' love because it is simply—love.

The interesting feature about the work is its naïveté, which is so happy and simple-minded; compare it with the 'domestic' or connubial love of *Ein Heldenleben*. Nevertheless, if its gentleness rather reminds us of *Paul et Virginie*, it is not frustrated like the similar simplicity of *A Village Romeo and Juliet* and Franck surely would never have seen the use of such a defeatist solution.

It is nice music to listen to.

Chapter Six

The Organ Works

FRENCH organ music contemporary with Franck was not of an uplifting character. The leading composers were men like Lefébure-Wély (1817-69) and Batiste (1820-76). The former was a virtuoso in his time and his music was always written with an eye to technique rather than to musicianship. The result was a plethora of pieces whose nature was exceedingly frothy and always brilliant—the congregation of St Sulpice can never have had a dull moment. If a comparison is made between virtuoso music written for piano and for church organ, the credit must be given to the latter because the player is usually hidden from the sight of his audience and the virtuoso fireworks are, therefore, aural rather than visual. Dr Percy Scholes suggests that were Lefébure-Wély living today he would qualify for the highest paid cinema appointment. Batiste was more clearly religious; sentimental, and easy to play, he commanded a following which could not rise to the heights demanded by the brilliance of Lefébure-Wély. Lemmens (1823-81), a Belgian, exercised considerable influence over the organists of his time all over Europe. His music was distinctly above the average, and his *Storm* is certainly the least objectionable of all such pieces, and their name used to be legion.

The influence which played the most important part in the outlook of Franck and others was that of Boëly (1785-1858) who was organist at St Germain l'Auxerrois. Boëly was a Bach enthusiast and therefore ploughed a lonely furrow; but he had followers who imitated his high ideals. Of these, Guilmant (1837-1911) and Saint-Saëns (1835-1921) were the most re-

95

nowned. The former, organist at the Trinité for many years, formed a repertoire of his own works chiefly designed for use with the Offices. His sonatas are marked by a sincerity and lack of show. This made them outstanding, but now they have faded out of knowledge and no longer occupy a prominent place in organ recitals. Their substance was never strong but at the time they appeared to be significant. The latter, for twenty years organist at the Madeleine, wrote most of his best and longest living music for the organ. It is all exceedingly well written and has the stamp of the skilled musician all over it. It consists of pieces rather than of works.

Slightly younger than these were Eugène Gigout (1844-1925) and Charles Marie Widor (1845-1937). The former was organist at St Augustin and founded an organ school. He was more of a virtuoso than Guilmant and Saint-Saëns and travelled much in this capacity. His organ music is solid and of considerably more substance than that of Guilmant. The latter held the appointment at St Sulpice from 1870 until his death, and succeeded Franck at the Conservatoire. His ten symphonies for organ will always be outstanding for their musicianship and masterly writing. In addition, he composed many orchestral works and wrote an excellent book on the orchestra.

The tradition in organ music, therefore, lay in a debased descent from Couperin. It was not taken very seriously by the faithful or by music lovers in general and was rather more part of the barrack-room furniture of the church than part of the church services.

It will be seen, therefore, that Franck played an enormously important part in the uplifting of the organ and its music, and although his influence was direct only on his immediate pupils and followers, his influence set the lead to other composers.

The progress of organ construction can easily be traced through the music written for it as each succeeding generation advanced in both fields. It would be quite impossible, of course, to play most of the virtuoso organ works of today on the organ at St Clothilde as it was in Franck's time, and the depressing thing is that, in the contrary direction, while it is possible to play Franck on a unit organ, the defects of the older instrument become even more apparent as the piece goes on. It must always be taken into account that the pulling-out and pushing-in of stops in Franck's day was a considerable matter, requiring time and strength; but this is no reason why the music should be spoken of derogatively. This attitude is unjust. Franck's organ music must be taken as it stands and as it refers to his own time. Some years ago there was a move to re-write Beethoven's horn parts and bring them up to date. The move did not get very far because it was felt that to carry out this scheme would be to alter something which was essentially Beethoven—but no one spoke disparagingly of Beethoven's music because of the limitation. With Franck the absolutely up to date mind finds anything suitable for flogging, and while even those who admire the music would be the last to admit it, they, also, qualify it in this manner.

Let us, therefore, say, once and for all, that the halting moments in Franck's organ music are usually caused by the exigencies of stop-changing, and have done with it. It is the matter, not so much the manner which concerns us.

The *Six Pièces d'Orgue* Op. 16 were written during his first years at St Clothilde when he found himself in command of an instrument far out-reaching the possibilities of anything which he had previously experienced. He was in his element, and not only was it worth his while to write music specially for that instrument, but he found a great deal of his impulse in the newness of the specification.

The first of these pieces is the *Fantaisie* (in C) major, a work very different from what the title might lead us to expect. Here are no fanfares, no rolling diapasons, no magnificent climaxes. The atmosphere throughout, except for one short episode, is tranquil and serene. The work is also notable because it proved Franck's ability to write 'scholarly music' and yet be primarily musical. It is in three main sections, each in ternary form, with a modulatory passage between the second and third. Each movement is in contrast to its predecessor; the first moves slowly and with dignity; the second is full of contrapuntal flow; the episode is rhythmic and emphatic, and reaches the highest dynamic, while the fourth is quietly chordal. The lyricism of the second has rarely been approached in organ music. The whole work fulfils the requirements of the cyclic form. The first movement does not get very much further from its tonic C than the subdominant F. After rather a static announcement of the opening tune, Franck indulges in his natural canonic writing, over which is played a theme reminiscent of the motive of 'Sleep' from *Siegfried* in this manner—up to this point the music has been identical without the countersubject.

Ex. 53

This coincidence is of no significance whatsoever. It has often happened. When Brahms wrote the second piano concerto in B flat, he said exactly the same as did Lalo in his G minor symphony, but in a different mode. The 'Brahms-Wagner' violin sonata is well-known. However, if the writer may quote a personal experience of his own, that these things happen (and every blockhead notices them, as Brahms said)—in 1947 he wrote the following little tune in an opera, *Conte Vénitien*.

Ex. 53A

Five weeks later he read M Leon Vallas's book on Vincent d'Indy. On page 139 there is a quotation in a footnote of exactly the same theme from an opera by Ernest Reyer called *Erostrate* of whose existence the writer solemnly swears that he had never heard.

There must be some kind of telepathy between composers of which they are unaware.

A reference to the opening theme, and the movement ends, to be linked with the following one by a passage which uses the convenient chord of the diminished seventh in order to reach the key of F minor—not a very extraneous modulation.

While being aware of the genius of a composer, there are moments in his music when one is made fully conscious of it. In the 'allegretto cantando' which comes now, we are not only made fully conscious of Franck's genius, but are convinced of it to such an extent that even if he had never approached the level in anything else, we should still use the term 'genius'.

The reason for this conviction is twofold. Here we have contrapuntal skill allied with intense musicality and that with the slenderest of means. Those who complain that only a Bach can be musical, and then not always markedly so, in two contrapuntal parts, should look at the seven pages which comprise this movement. There is something behind them of deep inspiration. It may be that Franck fought hard for the two invertible themes; that we know not, but the impression given is one of absolute spontaneity and inspiration. If the term 'seraphic' must be applied to Franck, then this movement can claim it. Here is the germ of the whole thing:

Ex. 54

'B' is placed at the top, as the theme of the middle section. Up to this point the modulations have not gone very far, but throughout this middle section the range is vast, including E flat minor, C sharp minor (by means of an enharmonic modulation) and F sharp minor, returning to F minor via D flat, again achieved enharmonically. An occasional passage such as this testifies to Franck's wide stretch, but otherwise the music is fluent and gentle.

Ex. 55

99

This music suggests a dim religious light, evening, with but a few candles burning, lofty arches and a high ceiling. It floats into all the corners of the building. This may be sentimental, but it describes the impression. The music itself, in actual fact, is far too beautiful to be sentimental.

A sixteen bar interlude uses a slight variation of Ex. 54 (B) in the pedals; it is chiefly characterized by the rhythm of its manual chords but, most significant of all, it is not in the four-bar phrase which we have by now learned to expect from Franck. An analysis of the rhythmic structure shows it to be two three-bar phrases followed by one of ten bars, so for once we break away from squareness.

The closing adagio is restful and serene. It is not till the last two lines that the pedals have a part independent of the left hand, and they punctuate the key with tonic and dominant 'quasi timpani'.

This section can easily be spoilt by adhering to the registration as indicated on the music. The Vox Humana is a stop of peculiarly penetrating quality which, unless properly voiced, can be exceedingly unpleasant. Continental organ builders take great care of this. Over here organists like to leave it alone, if they have any taste or unless the stop is exceptional. A literal following of the marked registration in French organ music is usually to be avoided because, like so many other things, their organs are not like ours. Fortunately the lovely second movement is marked as for a Flute stop.

There is little music as ineffably lovely as this *Fantaisie*. What did the other French organists of the day think of it?

Although the discarded thoughts of composers are best left alone, it may be of interest to say that the work caused Franck a lot of thought and trouble. The original MS has a long square chromatic movement of some twenty-seven bars length. It is mainly a dull succession of modulations. This came before the closing eight bars of the first section and explains the rather un-necessary link. There are also thirteen pages of very uninspired music which conclude with the opening sixteen bars, being followed by twelve bars of the second subject. The whole closes with a florid version of the opening theme. The entire section is in complete ternary form.

After its publication in the form we know, Franck still had doubts. A printed copy includes still another MS addition of seven pages inserted after the interlude at the end of the first section. It is based on the second subject which is used as a bass under choppy chords. There is a big climax on the second subject. The whole thing is Franck at his very worst. We must be grateful that better counsels prevailed.

The second piece is the *Grande Pièce symphonique*, a work of the magnitude and layout of a sonata. Vincent d'Indy singles it out in Vol. 2 of his *Cours de Composition musicale* and remarks its resemblance to the ancient Italian sonata by reason of the links joining up the several movements. It opens with an introduction, in Franck's favourite F sharp, in which the themes of the work are duly presented. The Allegro proper has for its material a theme of striking resemblance to that of the later symphony.

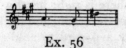

Ex. 56

This is played about with repetitively. The second subject in A major is chordal and hymn-like, without any of the future 'infinite melody' which Franck fell into so happily. The development does little but repeat the opening theme under a triplet right hand part which is neither dignified nor effective. The movement ends with a reference to the introduction. It is all rather dull.

The second movement in B major is different and is quite lovely in places. Franck was especially happy when soloing a moving tune over a quiet chordal left hand and pedals. The little theme has shape and covers a reasonable amount of ground. It leads straight into a scherzo, and here we have all the vices of French organ music—as *we* see organ writing. There is a lot of scampering about in semiquavers, and a very ordinary tune is played each side of a still more ordinary arpeggio figure.

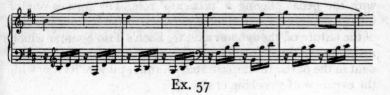

Ex. 57

French organists of the flashy type often indulge in this kind of thing and it is depressing to find the composer of the *Fantaisie* doing the same.

A reference to the Andante which precedes the Scherzo brings us to the finale. This has an introduction which ties up all the preceding themes and after a flourish or two the movement proper begins with a theme based on that of the first movement. There is a certain amount of effectiveness about this. It is rhythmic and the pedals have plenty to do, but the following fugato is not inspired.

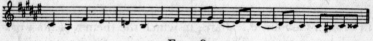

Ex. 58

In the final coda there is right hand writing which belongs more to the piano than the organ, and the layout in the original edition is particularly awkward to read when playing, albeit very clear when simply reading it.

Altogether this is a disappointing work. It is full of bombast and repeatedly lets us down because it never gets going. The only really satisfactory movement is the Andante. Particularly terrible is a left hand trill in the fugato section of the finale which looks as if Franck hesitated at sustaining an F sharp through three bars, which, incidentally, would have been very much better. It is awkward to play and dull to listen to.

The *Prélude, Fugue, et Variation* is loved by everybody. It has been arranged for several different instruments including piano solo (for which it is completely unsuited) and for piano and harmonium—Franck did this himself as the harmonium was an instrument which composers were trying to popularize at the time.

The texture of the whole work, except the link between the Prelude and the Fugue, is very slender, mostly in three parts, with the pedal playing a 'pizzicato' role. The tune is one of infinite tenderness and, *mirabile dictu*, it is a five bar phrase. It is of the nature of, though not akin to, Bach's Trio Sonatas which maintain the three part texture throughout but are interdependent in the parts. In simple ternary form, it pursues its way with the evenness of a rocking cradle.

Numéro d'ordre	Noms	Domiciles
1	*[Giacomo Meyerbeer]*	*[4 rue St. Augustin 49]*
2	*[F. Liszt]*	*[Rigole 19]*
3	*[signature]*	*[Ministère des Travaux publics]*
4	*[signature]*	*[Chargé d'affaires de Belgique]*
5	*[Auber]* — *Directeur du Conservatoire*	*[26 rue St. Georges]*
6	*[signature]* — *Professeur au Conservatoire*	*[34 St. Lazare]*
7	*[J. Bréton]* — *Membre de l'Institut*	*[40 Rue Richer]*
8	*[Urhan]*	*[3bis rue Richer]*
9	*[signature]*	*[38 rue de La Victoire]*
10	*[signature]*	*[24 r. d. Faubourg]*
11	*[Delaire]*	*[66 ...]*
12	*[L. Adam]*	*[3 r. Chopin]*
13	*[Lambert Massart]*	*[Rue St. Georges, 18]*
14	*[signature]*	*[24 r. Bellefond]*

First page of the subscription list for 'Trois Trios Concertantes'

Pastorale

(2nd time)

Ex. 59

The middle theme is syncopated.

The diapason link is founded on the opening theme, and tells us practically all that will happen in the Fugue. This link is but nine bars long. It may be straining a point, but the inclination cannot be resisted to point out that it is the answer to the fugue subject and not the subject itself which is given out in the link, by which the knowledgeable reader will realize that it is a tonal and not a real answer!

Here is no dashing virtuoso fugue with a striking subject which leaps and bounds. On the contrary it is one of the quietest and easiest to play in existence. It is seldom in four parts for more than a few bars and the stretti are in three parts only, which makes things much easier.

The Variation consists of left hand decoration. The theme is hardly varied at all in itself, the variation resting entirely in the left hand figuration. The pedals sustain pedal points for the most part although they play the middle theme for four bars.

This is one of the gems of organ music because it is so slight and so extremely pleasant to play.

So far so good; we have found two fine pieces and one indifferent one. No. 4 is most original in every way. Pieces with the title of *Pastorale* abound everywhere and offer little doubt in anticipation.

It is in three longish sections, of which the first consists of two periods.

Ex. 60

We get an anticipation of a semiquaver figure which later he was to turn to such great advantage in the first and third *Chorals*.

Ex. 61

This figure gives a fluttering poise effect to what otherwise would be an ordinary semiquaver passage.

The middle section shows us one of Franck's vices used advisedly, namely, that of centralizing a melody round a certain note, always returning to it and never straying very far away from it. Its connection with 'A' Ex. 60 is obvious.

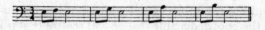

Ex. 62

This little passage becomes the subject of a smooth fugato section later on. The main material consists of crisp chords which must have sounded very clattering on the old organ action of St Clothilde—the writer remembers hearing it played on a modern electric organ and the clatter of the magnets almost drowned the music; the organist was using stops far quieter than was necessary.

Ex. 63

In the closing section, 'B' of Ex. 60 combines with 'A', making a charming combination of contrasting natures.

There are some works over which one's enthusiasms can get quite out of hand. This *Pastorale* is one of them. Not only is it original and unique, but it is so deft, so charming, and so exceedingly well done. Organists seem to revel in it, and no wonder.

It will be remembered that when Franck went in for the organ prize at the Conservatoire, his powers of invention so ran away with him that in one of the tests he could not stop. This seems to have happened with him in No. 5 of these *Six pièces d'orgue*, the *Prière*. The *Prière* is thirteen pages of good solid writing alternating with a chromatic melody over the inevitable triplet accompaniment. We here experience tentative Franck chromaticism and the piece has the air of an extended extemporization, with all the time in the world at the player's disposal. The piece contains many beauties, its main fault being that it is diffuse. Perhaps the dedication to Aristide Cavaillé-Coll made Franck determine that the organ for which it was written should have all its best points amply demonstrated.

It is in extended ternary form with interruptions, these being quasi-recitative passages which do nothing to contribute anything vital but serve both to hold up the unceasing movement and thin out the texture.

The main theme is thirty-two bars long. The music is harmonic and full of dignity, hardly prayerful, perhaps, but certainly purposeful. Starting in C sharp minor it does not progress far away from home. The second part of the theme is canonic between pedals and manuals and leads into rather a tortuous section which presages future complications. The second section consists of a tune over a triplet harmonic figure which suggests a lot of things but realizes none of them.

The path back to the tonic and the main theme is 'quasi recitativo' but does not seem to get anywhere. By his usual enharmonic means he gets into B flat minor and back to A major without any undue difficulty, and then follows an inexplicable link in octaves which is meaningless and ineffective. The second entry of the main theme is varied to the extent of having moving quavers all the time underneath it which get us into awkward double sharps.

Ex. 64

It is difficult to write of this *Prière* because it is so unequal. The main section is moving and sincere, but the middle and final ones seem to need string players. It is not good organ music because of the manual layout and the harmonic wobblings of the second section. As music it becomes wearisome in the middle, sags completely, then picks itself up again—to flop out once more at the end. Its difficulties are considerable, but they are difficulties of execution rather than of technique. One can imagine how it would sound in a non-resonant building at the hands of an inexperienced player with no smooth technique.

The last work, *Final*, is the only one to which the word 'cheap' can be applied. It opens with a jolly pedal solo which is jollier to play than to listen to, and then the manuals plunge into something which promises to go a long way but does not do so. Writing such as this is not very suitable for the organ, no matter how resonant the building.

Ex. 65

There is a good deal of passage work of a not very invigorating kind, and then the second subject leads us into a morass of accidentals. The key is Franck's favourite F sharp major, but instead of simplifying the notation, he must needs stick strictly to the letter, and we get a complication such as this which is sufficient to make a sight-reader's hair stand straight up on end, and even the first-class player is none too happy.

Ex. 66

The general effect of the rest of the piece is one of much ado about comparatively little, and not even the reiteration of the opening rhythm saves our interest.

It is interesting to note that of the six pieces, only three are perfectly satisfactory, and one nearly so. Each of the three is quiet. It is the noisy remainder that makes an assessment of Franck so difficult, even to his admirers. The excuse that they were his first serious organ ventures simply will not hold water because his practical experience should have taught him what he did not seem to know, namely, that the full organ can be equally the most dignified and the most vulgar sound on earth. Franck for some inexplicable reason seems to have avoided the former and fallen headlong into the latter.

Nevertheless, in the welter of nonsense and conventionality that was emanating from Parisian organ lofts every week, these pieces have something vital to communicate. In spite of their faults they are of the greatest importance in the panorama of music generally speaking; they said many things which were original and individual at their time, and still are so. In one sweep, they pointed a new approach and direction. In the case of the *Pastorale* there is no copy either in matter or manner.

The next organ works were not composed until 1878, fifteen years after the completion of the *Six Pièces*. This time there were only three and the general quality will be found to be different.

In the first place, the Franck idiom had been widened by experience. His harmonic thought had become deeper and increasingly chromatic. His sense of form, always strong, had become established; his melodic rhapsody had also acquired a wider curve. The first of these *Trois Pièces*, the *Fantaisie* (in A major) is a long work in which Franck did not altogether throw off the influences prevalent at the time. There seem to be one or two short cuts taken, which weaken the general dignity of the work. The opening theme is not notable for originality or space, but it served him well as the work proceeded.

True to previous practice he divides the main material into two contrasted periods, the first of which is in itself sectional in two-bar phrases of an arpeggio nature which always helps in the middle sections ; the second, moving in more conjunct motion, has flow and continuity.

Ex. 67

Although 'A' is used frequently as the work proceeds, sometimes in the treble, sometimes in the bass, sometimes as thematically independent, it never seems to get going and the general effect whenever it appears is to hold up the progress of the music. The great fault of this work is that it is altogether too sectional. Nothing is pursued to its logical conclusion—yet the material in many places is extremely beautiful. Whether Franck was experimenting in a free 'Fantasy' form is a question which can only be answered by personal opinion. The fact that there are three clearly defined main sections points to the fact that he had first-movement form at the back of his mind, but deliberately avoided a development in order to conform to the principles of freedom.

For the first time we find Franck using the reiterated chord of the *Pastorale* as a mere accompaniment. In the *Pastorale* it was all part and parcel of the thematic substance; here, and in the later *Pièce héroïque* it is simply an accompanimental figure. Over it, Ex. 67 'A' begins to suggest a melodic line.

Ex. 68

This attempt with the theme gets very little distance and it rarely leaves its dominant (E).

By and by a syncopated tune over another very ordinary figure heralds something of significance which we shall come across in the climax.

Ex. 69

Another 'seraphic' theme follows which is really beautiful and it is used more than once, but, in point of actual fact, not nearly enough.

Ex. 70

After discursive treatment of Ex. 67 'A' and the tune of Ex. 68, fragmentary and always trying to go somewhere or other, the climax is achieved rather arbitrarily and a straight forward announcement of Ex. 68 is played as a counterpoint to Ex. 67 'A' in the bass, each side of a detached left hand chordal accompaniment. This lasts for eight bars, and the position of the two themes is reversed. The third section immediately begins and covers the same ground as the exposition. The coda is exquisite and is built upon Ex. 70.

To analyse this work is disappointing because it does not do very much. To play it and to listen to it are different, and the ear does not mind the fragmentariness because of the lovely sounds. This, after all, is what really matters with music. Some find the work too long, others not long enough. It is much easier to play than many of the others and contains fewer Franckian awkwardnesses. Its general spirit is one of devotion and worship.

The *Cantabile*, which stands as the second piece of the three, is one long beautiful rapture. Here we seem to be in two worlds; the diapasons are prayerful while the main theme is that of *Les Béatitudes* in spirit. The Heavenly Voice seems to be speaking directly to His followers. Here are no accompanimental figures or clichés. Everything is thematic and continuous. The whole piece moves in one line with no haltings. Everything grows out of the opening germs and when one examines the piece, working backwards instead of forwards, there is hardly a passage which cannot be seen to have emerged from a previous fragment. Looking at it this way instead of the more normal method shows us the process much clearer.

Certain commentators have seen the influence of *Tristan und Isolde* in this piece, why or where it is difficult to find out. The chaste utterings of Franck's comfortable words are very far removed from the chromatic yearnings of Wagner's lovers.

Again, we have the opening material in two sections.

Ex. 71

Although 'A' may not look very promising and may seem to be but a succession of chords, notice that the bass is the opening of 'B'. The notes of the lower left hand are also used later on in the work, growing in this way.

Ex. 72

Particularly beautiful is the section beginning thus:

Ex. 73

The final coda is a slightly varied version of a fragment which has previously been heard in the pedals.

This lovely piece can rank with anything written by Bach. Here, in this comparison, we have the approaches of two different eras, one the direct expression of an historical fact, such as in the ineffable harmonization of the chorale *Christ lag in Tödesbanden* from the *Orgelbüchlein* with its suffering and subsequent glorification, the other an expression of thankfulness on the part of humanity, a thankfulness expressed with prayer and humility. 'I will not leave you comfortless' would seem to have been the spirit guiding Franck. It is not as serene as it is slightly fearful, as if He saw humanity driving to its own destruction regardless of His sacrifice. In spite of the chromaticism, it is neither sensuous nor sensual.

The *Pièce héroïque* is one of the most popular of Franck's organ pieces. It offers possibilities for enjoyable playing and the listener can get a kick out of the bluffness which characterizes the thought. We have repeated chords as an accompaniment and this time they are in keeping with the spirit of the material. The theme has boldness and is well built.

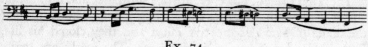

Ex. 74

Again the wide stretch of its composer makes for unnecessary difficulties. After a broad chordal section which is almost stirring, the writing descends to a Lefébure-Wély level of arpeggio figures more suited to the piano than the organ and there is another theme of the nature of Ex. 69 in the *Fantaisie* (in A major). A return to the opening theme leads us to some terribly static writing which looks as if it is meant to be impressive but in effect simply holds everything up. The 'hero' seems to be offering up some kind of prayer; but he does not do so for long, and once more there is some Lefébure-Wély writing in the left hand which simply does not lie anywhere near comfort. All this is rather perfunctory, particularly when we reach a heroic section over a tonic and dominant quasi-timpani pedal. Of interest are six bars which reverse the positions of the opening themes, to be repeated later when the climax is reaching its fruition.

At that fruition a distinctly vulgar atmosphere fills the work although it must be admitted freely that it comes off in performance, provided that one does not object to the organ being treated in this manner. The last page is one of dignity and triumph.

This is one of the first organ works which fulfils the requirements of the concert hall, and it will be remembered that Franck wrote the *Trois Pièces* for the new Trocadero organ, the presiding genius of which was Guilmant. Unfortunately it falls rather between two stools, being at moments distinctly and essentially 'churchy'—this is very obvious in the halting middle section. One wonders what the worldly Trocadero audiences thought of the *Fantaisie* and *Cantabile*. Did they heave a sigh when they found themselves more or less on their own ground in the *Pièce Héroïque*?

The *Andantino* (in G minor) was included in the original MS of the *Six Pièces* but Franck changed his mind and it was not published until 1889. It is a short piece with a trivial opening section which is relieved by a middle one of some dignity.

The *Trois Chorals*, however, are of a substance and inspiration which place them amongst the greatest music. They represent the acme of Franck's creative effort and they closed his life. Franck took no 'Chorale' as did Bach. The works are really Variations on a Theme—to call them 'Chorale-Preludes' is altogether wrong.

The first, in E major, has for its theme a long line of seven distinct periods, of which the third is a transposition of the first four bars of the first period. The periods pass freely through E minor, G major, E flat major, B major, G minor, E flat minor, G flat minor, B major, C sharp major, E major, A major, G sharp minor, F major, and finally back to E major, with several fleeting incursions elsewhere. Not bad for two and a half pages of manual writing throughout, but it all works out in the end. Everything sounds perfectly natural with the aid of the enharmonic change, and since the music is in clear four-bar phrases, any sudden change is smoothed over by the fact that the hands lift up from the keys and the ear starts again, so to speak. The seven periods commence as follows:

Ex. 75

The first variation is an ornamental version of No. 1.

Ex. 76

This ornamentation is placed in the tenor later on, under a fragmentary reference to the opening notes of No. 7. No. 5 is heard solo over a running semiquaver accompaniment. Finally, so far as this variation is concerned, the music is concerned with No. 7 between whose first and second stanzas the right hand refers to Ex. 75. Variation 2 is a typically Franckian discussion between two contrasted statements. A square harmonic emendation of No. 5 is interrupted by an important ornamented version of No. 4, important because the music deals with it for many pages to come and the opening plan of the theme is extended beyond measure.

We may refer to this extension as Variation Three. Here we have the fulfilment of the preceding variation. Over quiet and simple sustaining harmonies, the tune takes on ever increasing shape.

Ex. 77

At the thirteenth bar it becomes fragmentary and finally works into No. 4 which is perfectly unadorned. A brief link to the next variation is based on No. 1, and then No. 7 appears under Ex. 76.

Ex. 78

The position is reversed shortly after.

Ex. 79

A good climax is achieved by means of No. 1, and the music finally struggles into No. 7, chordally and with great triumph. The work ends with a reference to Ex. 76 on the full organ.

This is not only magnificently devised music, but it approaches greatness because of its beauty and sincerity. It is the Variation Form *par excellence* and is equalled only by the *Variations symphoniques* for piano and orchestra in sheer continuity and musical skill combined with deep creative instincts.

The second Choral, in B minor, is altogether different. Whereas the first was optimistic and generally serene and reconciled, the second is sombre and serious. It is in Passacaglia form, but there is no tiresome redundancy of theme which so often spoils even the best examples of its kind. Sometimes the theme is lost altogether, to return with renewed freshness. On these occasions there is completely new material which seems to have no thematic connection with anything else. Nothing grows out of the germ, as it does in the first Choral; it accumulates decoration and rhapsody about itself, and there is no struggle.

The theme is as follows:

Ex. 80

In the first variation the tune is placed in the top part, with regular chordal punctuation on the second and third beats. The pedal takes it up in Variation Two, under some awkwardly written manual harmonies. The second part of the theme then rises into the right hand doubled at the octave while left hand and pedals move in similar motioned chords. Down to the pedals again in Variation Three under triplet chords in the manuals. The same process as in the second, that of raising the second half of the theme into the right hand is carried out, and we move straight into something quite new and quite different. The spirit of the A major *Fantaisie* now takes a hand but the resemblance is suggestive rather than direct.

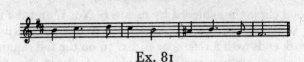

Ex. 81

This is followed by an interlude of running semiquavers in which the diminished seventh plays a great part, and this conversation between two ideas continues for some while.

Then we arrive at one of those dramatic interludes which are so difficult to make convincing. Loud cadenza-like passages interspersed with reflective writing close the devotional effect of Ex. 81 and the Passacaglia theme returns once more, in G minor. Here it is in the right hand and from this point the music flows smoothly, the theme going into the pedals and then in an inside part, without any interruption or halting. Mention must be made of the figure accompanying the first reappearance of the tune as it becomes thematic, towards the end.

Ex. 82

The seraphic writing of Ex. 81 returns and is dealt with at some length, passing easily from E flat minor to F sharp minor. It is now that we get the growth of Ex. 82 which appears first unadorned, and gradually becomes intensified by decorative semiquavers. There is a feeling of uncertainty and restlessness as the music moves steadily onwards to its climax and then the theme itself is stated in fifteenths, the first part being in the treble, and the second in the bass, the reverse of the previous process. The Choral ends quietly with a variant of the second half of the theme.

This has never attained the popularity of the other two because in the first place, it is the hardest to play, and, in the second, altogether more serious. Many consider it the finest of the three.

The third, in A minor, is the most played and superficially the most attractive; this does not gainsay its quality which is well up to the standard of the others. It is altogether more lyrical and if not quite so resigned as the first, it is full of a happy optimism.

The Choral theme does not appear for some while. Franck establishes what is a theme and at the same time an accompaniment right at the beginning, in some semiquaver arpeggio writing of the broken chord variety. This will be found to be very convenient for combining with the main theme because of its chordal nature.

Ex. 83

A passage of great dignity brings us to the choral.

Ex. 84

The opening figure now becomes of thematic importance. This is not the kind of organ writing which we, in this country, consider suitable for the instrument, but the French have always had a liking for it.

These Chorals, as we have said, were Franck's last works and it is fitting that the very last of all should contain what follows next, because of all Franck's melodies it is one of the most lyrical and rhapsodic. It has shape and length and if not quite in the category of 'infinite melody' approaches it nearly.

Ex. 85

In its extension Franck uses the figure mentioned in connection with the *Pastorale* which gives it a poised and fluttering effect.

Ex. 86

A reference to the opening bars of the Choral brings us to a
new section in which Ex. 85 alternates with each line of the
Choral. The hands both go on to the Great Organ and Ex. 86
carries us on to a climax which dies down on a mediant pedal
point to a resumption of the opening matter. Shortly afterwards
the Choral is heard at the top, in the key of G sharp major over
a pedal point on the flattened seventh (F sharp). It descends to
G major, the pedal point now being the flattened seventh in that
scale. The music is quiet but greatly disturbed. Eventually the
Choral emerges (if it had ever vanished) in extenso over a complete statement, literally, of the opening broken chord figure, on
full organ. The closing coda is tremendous.

Thus is completed the gamut of Franck's major organ works,
and these *Trois Chorals* are a fitting swan-song of one who strove
to the utmost of his ability to give only of his best.

Mention must be made of a set of *Pièces Posthumes* for Harmonium or ordinary Organ. Most of these date from 1858 to
1863. In the majority of cases it had been better to have left
them alone. Composers invariably leave behind them a number
of MSS which they have felt not worthy of publication but have
not had the courage to destroy; short pieces written down
quickly for some particular occasion, perhaps for some pupil or
other who wanted something to play 'at our church'. This collection is described as 'pour l'office ordinaire' and the clue here
is that Franck felt they might be useful for village organists—a
number of French composers have made such collections. There
are very few which reflect credit on their composer.

Again, it is the quiet pieces which are the best, and the noisy
ones in this collection are of a vulgar nature which had best be
forgotten; yet even some of these have their moments, but they
let us down horribly at others.

The meditative pieces which are useful today are of no very
great originality. They have their counterpart in similar 'Com-
munions' and 'Offertoires' by composers like Guilmant but lack

Guilmant's sweetness and sentimentality. An *Elévation* in E has considerable beauty in its quiet way. Apart from a few bars of arpeggio padding it is concise and thoroughly satisfying. This is dated 29th October 1859. An unnamed and undated piece in A flat is also acceptable but has not the flow of the previous *Eléva-tion*. The gem is the *Offertoire pour la Messe de Minuit*, dated 1st December 1858. This is perfectly beautiful and in it there are traces of the future Franck of the Chorals. It is very effective even though its effect is obtained by a low pedal D which on the 32ft stop always convinces. It is religious music and exactly the type which places everything in the right atmosphere. It is written on two distinct themes which appear twice each, with coda, again on a low pedal D. It is the music of one who believed absolutely in the Sacrifice and who was filled with an holy joy. It may not be strikingly original now—one can think of a good many similar pieces written since, and possibly with no know-ledge of the ancestry—but it is sincere.

Of the noisy pieces, an *Offertoire* in F minor (undated) which opens the volume is full of suggestions of the future Franck because of its modulations. A nine page *Offertoire* which begins in G minor and ends in D major is vigorous and with some pruning should be useful for a Festival voluntary. It is undated. For the rest, the book consists of short interludes and harmoniza-tions of the *Gloria* which village organists might indeed find handy. On the whole it would have been better if a selection had been made rather than publication of the whole.

A better collection is that known as 'L'Organiste' which con-sists of fifty-nine pieces written on two staves for use with har-monium. These pieces were as much as Franck could remember of the many versets he extemporized for the Magnificat. He hoped to write a hundred of them but death interrupted the plan. The MS of the set begins very methodically and neatly but by the time he reached the fortieth his illness had taken a firm hold of him and the remainder are written in pencil, very roughly.

What applies to the previous set applies here in large measure. The quieter ones are infinitely superior to the noisy, but in general there is no sense of completion. The pieces were intended for the use of parish organists whose powers of extemporization were limited. For this reason *L'Organiste* had its value as it was the first attempt to fill a deficiency which has had many successors. None of the pieces have titles and the same theme may be heard in several.

Amongst the MSS in the Bibliothèque Nationale is a *Grand Choeur* written very untidily on villainous green paper. It is written on three staves and, therefore, was obviously intended for organ and not harmonium. It might be termed 'a useful voluntary'. Franck seems to have been passing through a financial crisis during its composition. On odd pages there are some frenzied financial problems worked out, one of which proves that if 10,000 francs are added to 90,000 francs, the result is 100,000 francs.

The influence of Franck's organ music is seen in the symphonies and collections of pieces by Louis Vierne who used much of Franck's particular layout, particularly his use of a theme over a steadily flowing left hand accompaniment. However, it completely by-passed Widor whose symphonies are of the type emanating more from the École Niedermeyer than from St Clothilde.

It is not without significance that we have found Franck to be at his best in the quiet works and not in the noisy. In the study of the orchestral works and of *Les Béatitudes*, it is obvious that when delineating something either demoniacal or satanic, he failed because he could not bring himself to realize the potentialities of evil in its strongest forms. His technique and idiom were not of that ilk. Consequently when he wished to be ebullient he usually became commonplace, always excepting the three great Chorals which we have found to be of outstanding quality, and when the powers of evil demanded his attention, he expressed them in an almost childish tongue.

The significance of his organ music is that it raised the instrument from being a cross between a mere adjunct to the sentimental moments of the Mass and a virtuoso machine. The descent from Bach is shown very clearly here. Together with Guilmant and Saint-Saëns, he altered a whole attitude. That there are moments when he seems to be extemporizing is a failing common to most composers of organ music whose routine work entails much of this.

If he did not write a fugue comparable with any single one of the Bach tradition, he did transmute the Bach approach to organ music. To compare the two is absurd, if we do so by placing work against work; but if we do so on the lines of achievement, then Franck in his day and in his way accomplished as great a work as did Bach. The true Bach enthusiast cannot blink his eyes to certain weaknesses and dullness. The true Franck enthusiast cannot do so either to such things as the *Grand Pièce Symphonique*, the *Final* and even the *Pièce Héroïque*, but no lapses in either composer can detract one tittle from the glory of the whole.

Franck outshone his contemporaries by his seriousness. Guilmant's organ music has an air of utility, being always well attached to its purpose; Saint-Saëns's is completely detached from the service; it is more for the odd voluntary or recital than for anything else. Franck seems to be in the Presence in every bar, even in the *Pastorale* which nevertheless is a thank offering for the gifts of nature. We can imagine the congregation at the Trinité finding Guilmant's music a religious assistance and that at the Madeleine sitting back and losing all connection with the previous sacrament. At St Clothilde it was only the musically inclined who 'stayed to listen' at the end of the service, although all must have been completely swayed by the devotional extemporizations which they had heard during the service.

Even in his weakest pieces there is always an absence of flippancy in Franck's organ music. The term 'light' can be applied only to the *Pastorale* and the *Prélude, Fugue, et Variation* and then only because they attempt to probe no depths or express a higher thought in the way that the C major *Fantaisie* rose above this world in its entirety, and the *Cantabile* also. These last two works are amongst the most inspired and beautiful in organ literature, the first for its simplicity, and the second for its well-wrought harmonies. The Chorals will never be equalled.

We may wonder what Franck was like as an organist. Maurice Emmanuel says that he was a better pianist. Emmanuel goes further and says that Franck thought too often in terms of the piano when writing his left hand passages. That he was a marvellous extemporizer is undisputed; hence he must have been an excellent church organist without necessarily being a recitalist. He sat at the console for some minutes collecting his thoughts, then, without any hesitation, plunged into the most wonderful improvizations. He played with dignity—perhaps the whole matter may be summed up in Maurice Emmanuel's words, 'A sa tribune, Franck était Roi'.

According to Vincent d'Indy he was always distressed when the Sanctuary Bell told him that the Offertory was finished. 'But I have not said anything yet' or 'What a pity'. Maurice Emmanuel confirms this, and says that Franck never continued after the appointed time. On the other hand, Gabriel Pierné has a long account (related in the *Musical Times*) of the difficulties the clergy got into because Franck would not stop, being oblivious of everything except his thoughts. Pierné tells of an elaborate system of bells in the Sanctuary, an electric bell in the organ loft, and even the sending up of a Server.

At the organ Franck forgot everything, his neglect as a composer, the petty jealousies of the other musicians, if, indeed, he ever realized the latter. At the moment of Elevation he always left the organ stool to make his reverence and then resumed his playing. There was no talking in that organ loft, no behaviour as if it were something unrelated to the proceedings at the other end of the church. The well-known painting by J. Rongier shows Franck in the act of drawing a stop which seems to be coming out by the yard. It shows his finely tapered fingers poised over the keys and his expression is of one lost to the world.

Photos of organists in action are often unconvincing and give no sense of movement or action. A remarkable one appeared in a musical journal many years ago of Sir Walter Parratt playing the Psalms at St George's, Windsor—with not a single stop drawn. This painting of Franck has life and reality.

At the time of the centenary, *Comoedia* published a remark made to a visitor to St Clothilde by the Curé, to the effect that the organ was in a bad state, but the organist was a very old man and things would be different when his successor arrived. This has a certain significance....in two directions.

Chapter Seven

The Chamber Works

THE three *Trios concertans* for piano, violin and cello, which constitute the official Op. 1 of César Franck were published by Schlesinger of Paris and Schuberth of Hamburg and Leipzig. The copies in front of me bear the imprint of a rubber stamp with the composer's full names—'César Auguste Franck de Liége'—surrounding a lyre. The dedication to 'Sa Majesté Leopold 1er, Roi des Belges' fills the centre of the title page which includes a print of the royal crown. The works, however, remained Franck's property, the address being Rue Laffitte 43, Paris.

The earliest works of any composer must of necessity bear the imprint of their ancestry, this ancestry not necessarily being that most popular at the time but showing the favourites of the writer at that particular period. There are few such works which in the light of maturity have anything but an historic interest. It is usual to see in them signs of that maturity, but there are exceptions, and Franck is amongst them, in every respect save one.

To perform these works in all seriousness today would be ludicrous if not to say amusing (in the true sense of the word). They are too clearly immature and altogether too much of their period. Nevertheless, we must remember once again that Franck had no French tradition to fall back upon. Chamber music was almost non-existent in France at the time; the German models which he studied were indisputably the best in the world but not in any way suited to the Gallic temperament. We can see, therefore, a not inconsiderable amount of enterprise in these youthful works, but it is more in the construction than in the inspiration or technique. Franck's genius in regard to form makes him a figure of paramount importance, and remembering that both our living authorities deny any influence from either Reicha or Leborne, it cannot be denied that from the first his mind sought out fresh moulds, and in these Trios formulated the structure of the later Symphony and other works.

The points of contact between these first and the mature works are largely found in their form, but the essence of a certain aspect of Franck melody, the fondness for a centralizing note, and its repetition, are apparent in the very first bars of the very first Trio. The cyclic outlook is found in its embryo, but particularly in the original last movement of the third Trio, which was later issued as a separate work.

The connection with other composers is most interesting, for it was undoubtedly Schumann who governed his piano thought, not Beethoven, whose works he studied with the greatest care. Most curious of all are certain pianistic twists which sound like Brahms. The Trios were published in 1841—Brahms's first published work is dated more than ten years later. No study of Brahms ever mentions Franck, and it is extremely unlikely that Brahms, when he started as a composer, had ever heard of him, far less of his music. Perhaps Liszt had mentioned Franck's name. Liszt was generous in this respect and never kept a discovery to himself. Perhaps he showed the Franck Trios to Brahms, but by the time the two had become even passingly friendly, Brahms had already launched himself on his career. We may take it that the 'King of Sixths' as Dame Ethel Smyth so thoughtlessly dubbed Brahms to his face (thereby causing the great man some discomfort) was completely unaware of Franck when he wrote his first works and when Vincent d'Indy took him a copy, many years later, of Franck's *Rédemption*, with the composer's homage, Brahms put it aside on a chair without comment. Whether Brahms had by this time found out that certain points of his technique were not as individual as he thought they were, and was accordingly piqued, we shall never know, and it signifies only to the extent that the whole thing reveals interesting individuality on the part of a young Belgian composer.

No matter what Franck's father may have had in mind regarding the future of his son, that son paid little heed to it when composing these works, for in no place can we detect the basis of virtuosity for its own sake in the writing for any of the instruments, although there are occasional outbursts of pianism.

The Trios offer certain points of interest, although their content is not very striking. Certain salient features are common to all. For example, there is little, if any, modulation. Franck chromaticism had not yet been born, and an excursion to the dominant is about the furthest any movement goes. The melodies do not move very far afield and there is a good deal of padding.

On the other hand, the form is strikingly enterprising and prophetic, and when we reach what is now called the fourth Trio, but which, nevertheless, was the last movement of the third, we find ourselves in front of something if not quite original, certainly not in common practice. In the recapitulation section the second subject comes before the first, thus forming a kind of façade in which each theme stands opposite itself on each side of the arch. Mozart did this. Today some composers, particularly Arthur Honegger, show a tendency towards it because of its logic, and for the fact that it avoids complete and exact repetition of design. Franck himself did not use it again, and this stands as the one example of an enterprise which was to have very few repercussions, if any at all, until the twentieth century.

The First Trio, in F sharp—even at that early age Franck was attracted by this key—gives us the cyclic form very clearly. The work is based upon two generative themes, one static and the other correspondingly mobile.

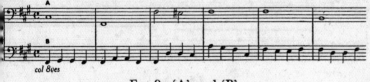

Ex. 87 'A' and 'B'

'B' presages much of the future Franck, the 'Finale' of the *Prélude, Aria, et Final* and the Quartet particularly. Vincent

125

d'Indy sees in this theme merely a convenient countersubject, but it is too prominent, too significant to be so relegated. The main idea of the movement other than 'B' is the following melody which suggests the regularity of many future themes, the Symphony, *Psyché*, not infinite by any means, but absolutely flowing and unrhythmic.

Ex. 88

This is the basis of the scherzo which was two trio sections. The second of these is prophetic of Brahms—the slowly rising dotted minim chords on the piano, for example, while the next example is only a little less rugged than much of Brahms's habitual piano writing when excited.

Ex. 89

The finale, in first-movement form, is uncompromising, but suggests that the young brain was not yet developed.

Generally speaking this Trio is the most successful of the three. True, its influences are easy to see. Writing like this might have come from almost any Schumann work.

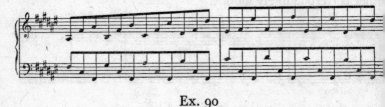

Ex. 90

However, in it are some of the germs of the future Franck which become apparent only in the light of maturity. At first glance they suggest nothing outstanding.

The Second Trio bears the description *Trio de salon*. It is the least interesting and says comparatively little. Now and again we think we are listening to Brahms:

Ex. 91

but otherwise there is nothing to note except a freer use of the instruments, in imitation. Performance today would be intolerable.

The Third is dramatic and the writing is more sure. The instruments keep their interlocking independence much more firmly and the writing throughout is well knit. The piano is used in an almost bravura style. For many bars on end there is a reiterated octave, rather in the manner of Schubert's *Erl King*, which requires an iron wrist and inflexible control. In this work more than in either of the others does the fingerprint of the future Brahms appear. We are tempted to quote one or two examples.

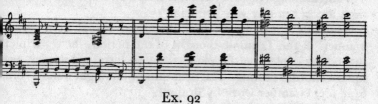

Ex. 92

An appalling piano figure of the chop-stick variety mars many pages and a long stretch of chordal trills completely spoils some impassioned string writing. Nevertheless, of all the three Trios, this is one which could be played today if only to point to the astonishing prophecies which it contains; this performance would include the final last movement, not the original one which constitutes Trio No. 4.

The enterprise of this young composer in the early twenties who preferred chamber music to the more showy orchestra with which to appear before the world as a composer, and at a time when chamber music had sunk into oblivion as far as French composers were concerned, is much to be commended. That his technique and inspiration were not strong enough to carry him through the task is no point against him.

The Fourth Trio shows an astonishing revivification of Franck's young energies. Towards the middle of the third Trio it looks as if he had almost written himself out; in the fourth movement all his energies returned and there is much thought behind it. Its enormous length fully justified Liszt's advice to issue it as a separate work, but, what is more important, we find in it the first complete cyclic form and the work (as such we will call it) springs from the opening germ. The entire theme is quoted because it is another instance of the first use of a feature which became part and parcel of the Franck technique, namely, letting a theme grow out of itself.

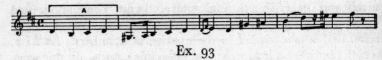

Ex. 93

All through the work the entire melodic thought springs from 'A', and although its progression is of short duration, the derivations are not in any way artificial.

Generally speaking we find the usual efforts at a 'grand manner' in the Teutonic thought of the period—heavy triplets two octaves apart on the piano through sustained strings, and square chordal writing. The next quotation might almost come from any chamber work by Brahms.

Ex. 94

The pianism shows its first Franckian individuality:

Ex. 95

while the closing Coda presages the coda of the Violin Sonata.

Ex. 96

In the Franck canon this work marks the last Teutonic influence in the published works, further reason for the decision not to publish *Ce qu'on entend sur la montagne*. From this moment Franck lightened his style with a clearly defined Gallic spirit and nowhere else can we find any influence of Schumann or Franck's other German idols. It would be interesting if there were some evidence of Brahms having come across these Trios in his youth —his first published work was the C major Piano Sonata, dated 1853. The basis of Ex. 94 was considerably enlarged upon by Franck in the new finale to the third Trio and the fact that the Trios were published by a German publisher may have made

I

them accessible to Brahms. None of the Brahms authorities make any reference to the visit of Vincent d'Indy.

The Piano Quintet was composed from 1878 to 1879, and Franck was in no hurry over it. Twenty-six years, therefore, elapsed between the Trios and this work.

By the time Franck set out on the composition of this work he had formulated his style and had no doubts as to where he was going. The cyclic form had for him become the natural means of expression and his instinctive knowledge and skill in variation made it perfectly logical. The Piano Quintet is the first complete example of his use of the form. From the very first to the very last bar of each movement and, indeed, of the whole work, cohesion and continuity are thus maintained, and the derivations are clear. With the Brahms F minor, Franck's work is a standard example.

The difficulty with chamber music using the piano today is that it has associations which disturb the seriousness of listening. To the older generation, for example, the people now in their fifties, the effect of strings playing in unison with piano arpeggio accompaniment is reminiscent of the silent films. At moments of stress the old chamber music combinations of the cinemas invariably soared about in this manner. The younger generation finds itself reminded of the hundreds of 'light orchestras' which play in restaurants and on the radio.

From the composer's angle, the chief difficulty is the avoidance of too easy conventionalities of piano writing and the temptation to let the other instruments play too subordinate a part in the ensemble. Franck carefully studied the available works. Doubtless he saw the perils of the Schumann Quintet, how it attempted too much and so often made the piano too prominent.

The germ of the material of the Quintet appears right from the first when the opening with all its dramatic force and simplicity gives the listener the first thrill.

Ex. 97

The whole work is derived from the falling fragment 'A', and the semitone occurs at the beginning of every theme, often inverted.

The forceful introduction leads straight into the Allegro proper, 'A' now having this shape:

Ex. 98

In the second half we have the typical Franck way of extending and enlarging a tune, making it rise higher with each variation.

It is a long way to the second subject and during the connecting episode the germ goes through permutations such as these:

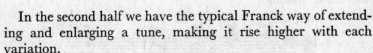

Ex. 99 'A', 'B', and 'C'

Of these 'B' is more incidental than actually thematic.

The second subject is derived from 'C', the four opening bars being an exact transposition. All through the movement we are constantly aware of the importance of the germ particularly in its relationship to the principal subject (Ex. 98). Never once does it halt; towards the approach of the long coda there is an interesting antiphonal passage between strings and piano which anticipates certain moments in the Symphony. It is worth noticing in connection with this work and the *Prélude, Choral et Fugue* how subconsciously Franck was working towards the Symphony and how related in so many little ways the three works are to each other.

The whole of the development section of this movement is one long breath, as it were. The material is expanded and extended and the fragments are combined and treated canonically in a manner without parallel since Beethoven. Not even Brahms was so unified.

The second movement, whose principal theme is Ex. 1 (in Chapter Four), is in simple 'lied' form, very tender and sincere. It is a clear example of inspiration which, although full of feeling, avoids sentimentality. At the climax there is the following interesting writing.

Ex. 100

Relation to the Finale is established at the beginning of the connecting episode, with this fragment.

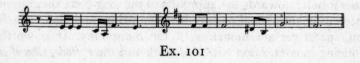

Ex. 101

Its corresponding derivation is anticipated for convenience' sake.

The instruments are written for in a very comprehensive manner. There is plenty of variety and the conversational moments are charming. The piano writing is typical Franck without any undue difficulties. There is more cohesion here than in the first movement because there is less reason for discourse. Although there are quite a number of stretches either for piano alone or piano and one other instrument in the first movement, here the forces are treated more as a group. It is the music of a contented mind which had found its justification and whose touch and means of approach were absolutely sure.

The Finale opens with a long introduction which might almost be considered a Scherzo in itself, save that the effect is always one of pressing on instead of something definite. The principal subject, when eventually it does grow out of the introductory matter, is rather different from anything we have so far heard.

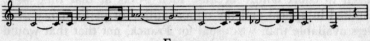

Ex. 102

The second subject is the second part of Ex. 101.

Most interesting is the coda built upon Ex. 99 'C' in triple time which thus sets the seal upon the complete unity of the work. This unity, which is maintained so consistently, precludes performance of any movement separately except the first.

A noteworthy feature of the melodies is the tendency to drop a third. This finds its culmination in the Violin Sonata which we shall discuss next, but it is not as significant an anticipation as the examples suggesting the Symphony.

Its first performance staggered the audience. Saint-Saëns who played the piano part—why was it that he so often played music which he hated?—was overcome with its passion and considered that it was very much overdone. Franck dedicated the work to him, thus unsuspectingly heaping coals upon coals of fire on his rival's head. The best reaction to the work was the remark of Delaborde who, after hearing it, turned to those round him and said 'Le père Franck me ravage.'

It is not a work to be taken in hand lightly or unadvisedly.

Franck makes great demands upon his players. Imagination and a perfect ensemble are paramount. They are particularly necessary in the lyrical slow movement whose beauties are so great that nothing but perfection should result. Franck was wise to wait until his technique had matured before tackling chamber music.

Up to this point we have noticed that the element lacking in Franck's melodic stream is that of pure lyricism. It is only in the slow movement of the Quintet that it has been at all obvious. We now reach that part of our study in which we find the melodic essence to be pure lyricism and, as a result, the work in question is one which not only is approved by Franck's general detractors but is almost universally loved.

Franck's friendship with Eugène Ysaÿe was bound to lead only to one end, to the composition of a work designed especially for him. To have written a Violin Concerto would have been to court failure because such works at that time were limited in appeal and the opportunities for performance even less available than was usual for Franck, not that that would have worried him. He turned to the Sonata as a means of giving the distinguished Belgian violinist a work which he could include in his regular repertoire.

Having established his thought in the cyclic form through the Quintet, Franck had no difficulty in using it for this work. In the Quintet there was a tendency to make use of the interval of the falling third. In this Sonata the interval is the governing factor of the principal themes. The work grows out of the principal theme, itself built upon the chord of the dominant ninth, and the closing bar of that theme.

Ex. 103 'A' and 'B'

The only other theme which has no connection with this germinal is the second subject of the first movement and even this will be seen to form the cell for certain short passages which are sometimes part of a fragment of a theme.

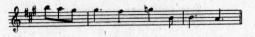

Ex. 104

The work, therefore, will be found to be cyclic throughout.

Ex. 103 'A', being chordal, offers opportunities for canonic writing of which Franck takes little advantage, the process being much too obvious.

The first movement is concerned with statement and restatement of these themes in modified Sonata Form. The general trend of the music is one of complete calm.

The second movement, marked 'Allegro' conceals its theme in some subtle pianism, the theme germinating from Ex. 103 'B'. It is not till the violin enters that it declares itself.

Ex. 105

It leads into the second subject through a derivation of Ex. 103 'A' which later plays a very important role.

Ex. 106

The actual second subject, based on Ex. 103 'B' has length and breadth.

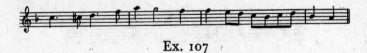

Ex. 107

In itself it forms the substance of a link which holds up the onward rush of the music and prevents the movement being a breathless clatter.

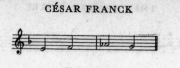

Ex. 108

Pianists have a field day in this movement and although the music is almost virtuosic, it never obscures the violin part. Such canonic writing as this needs careful control.

Ex. 109

The third movement, styled 'Recitativo-Fantasia', is a complete résumé of the material which has already appeared. Ex. 17 'A' comes in in these three ways.

Ex. 110 'A', 'B' and 'C'

Ex. 108 is not forgotten and it becomes the theme over some broken chord pianism. A new theme which can be just related to Ex. 108 makes a brief appearance:

Ex. 111

to be followed by another which passes insignificantly at this particular moment, to play a big part in the fourth movement.

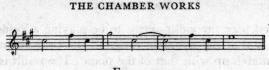

Ex. 112

Ex. 103 'A' is referred to momentarily in the course of the material, but any tendency to regard every leap of a third in either direction as emanating therefrom must be checked. The next example is fully justifiable from this point of view, however.

Ex. 113

The movement dies down, and without a break we go straight into the finale which is one of those movements of universal appeal which suffer from its players. The descent of the principal subject is open to the imagination but we may allow that it springs from Ex. 103 'A'. The writing is canonic throughout and the two instruments proceed on their way discursively and gently, the piano always being 'dux'.

Ex. 114

At the close of this conversation, the violin plays a long stretch of equal quavers above a complete form of Ex. 111. The piano is extremely static and the episode can be said just to convince provided the violin murmurs sufficiently unobtrusively.

Ex. 113 returns in C sharp major, to be followed by Ex. 112 with the positions reversed, the piano having the moving quavers and the violin the theme.

Another exposition of the principal subject in E major follows and then we come to a passage of considerable power in which for the first time the violin seems to be playing a losing battle. The fact is that the dynamic range of the instrument cannot possibly match up with that of the piano. The result is slightly vulgar and commonplace no matter to what extent the pianist keeps himself back.

A new episode appears, founded on Ex. 106 which gives an entirely new viewpoint over a restless and excited piano.

The third and fourth bars of Ex. 114 form a link between a quiet hint at the principal subject passing through the keys of B flat minor and major, and E flat major. There is some ingenuity here, for the latter progression consists of the first two bars of the principal subject, the theme being thus completed by a complete section in itself. Ex. 111 reappears and then the position of the first and second subjects is reversed for the final section. The second subject comes in boldly in the key of C major dovetailed on to the previously mentioned piano link.

The principal subject re-enters in its original form and the work finishes with one of those unfortunate codas for which Franck and his period were so famous. The vulgarity of this is usually enhanced by the lack of restraint shown by the pianist and the energy displayed by the violinist to keep his end up. It is a coda of this nature which forbids our regarding the work as a complete model.

Nevertheless, this Sonata is a classic. Its serenity is charming; even the riotous second movement is more high-spirited than turbulent. Its very tunefulness gives it a unique character because it is never trivial and although perfectly serious music, is never prosy or pretentious. There is no padding anywhere and this is the result of the cohesive nature of the cyclic form which, to be consistent, must lead from one importance to another without any extraneous material, for while even the links are thematic, there can be nothing ulteriorly introduced.

The original sketches for the String Quartet show that Franck had considerable difficulty in making a satisfactory beginning and even when he had got really started, it all gave him a great deal of thought, with the exception of the Scherzo which appears to have been written in ten days.

When Schumann decided to write his first string quartet he shut himself up for days with Beethoven's works in the same genre. Franck did the same, but did not confine himself to Beethoven. Vincent d'Indy tells how for some time they saw the table littered with string quartets of all kinds, but, being wise, put two and two together without making any inquiries. Eventually the Quartet took definite shape.

The actual start of a work always gives composers the greatest amount of trouble. The achievement lies in the fact that the final result shows no trace of difficulty. Franck made two attempts at the initial introduction before he was satisfied with a third. It may be of interest to quote the three successive versions of the first six bars—for once the rhythmic structure is not that of four bars.

Ex. 115 'A', 'B' and 'C'

The germinal idea is contained within the first three bars of 'C'. The introduction is in lied form and is complete in itself. The allegro has for its theme this vigorous little tune:

Ex. 116

139

The connecting episode introduces a melody which will be found to play an important part in the finale:

Ex. 117

while the second subject is as insignificant as was the first prominent:

Ex. 118

The development section begins with a fugato on the germinal idea, in the key of F minor, and then plunges straight into the material of the exposition. This is fevered music ever impelling itself onwards. Just before the coda, we have unorthodox writing of this nature which descends from similar passages in the Symphony:

Ex. 119

The coda is a truncated repetition of the introduction in D major, bringing the movement to a quiet finish.

The Scherzo which follows is ethereal in its fancifulness and gives the impression of having been written straight off. It is not unlike *Les Éolides* in spirit and this fragment is closely akin to that work.

Ex. 120

Not that Franck repeated himself in any way, but his individual shapes were very much his own.

A quiet trio section forms the basis of the coda to the movement.

Vincent d'Indy says that the slow movement gave Franck more trouble than any other part of the work. Like Beethoven he sweated and toiled until he was satisfied. The result proved that perspiration is indeed the handmaid of inspiration and in all great music gives no hint at itself. This beautiful music, serene yet impassioned, deeply felt and wrought, full of intensity, is consistently sustained in all its moods. It is quartet writing *par excellence*. The four instruments are used as a body without relief, yet we are never conscious of any feeling of oppression. It is no hymn and it is not 'seraphic'. It is, on the contrary, the outpouring of a very human mind, a mind in touch with realities in spite of its ideals. It is 'absolute' music, like the Symphony. No literary or pictorial basis can be read into it anywhere, yet it is full of imagination. To write a great slow movement is a test for any composer, for it is here that his ability to make us enter into his thoughts either stands or falls, and there can be no padding to help us along. This movement is as great as any of the slow movements of the later Beethoven, Schubert, and Brahms. That it was successful at its first performance proved that at last Franck had persuaded his hearers of the sincerity of his inspiration.

The finale is a mighty edifice built up with the bricks and mortar of the previous movements. Commencing with a reference to the previous themes it never strays away from them. It is here that Ex. 117 makes itself felt.

Ex. 121

The germinal idea is used to its fullest extent in both major and minor modes and the music moves along in a sea of optimism.

Had Franck written nothing else but these three chamber works they would have entitled him to rank among the greatest composers. If it was in truth his mission to raise the position of music in France and to place it on a level with that of every other country, then he succeeded. These chamber works were laid on the foundations of the greatest classical traditions. There is no other composer who might have written them and nowhere do they show any signs of slavish copying of the models, models which every composer must have in his mind. In the same way that he taught his pupils by the examples of the great masters, so he taught himself.

Chapter Eight

The Piano Works

O F Franck's boyhood works for piano, only the *Première Grande Sonate*, written at the age of thirteen, is of any interest. The previous work, composed when he was eleven and a half was simply a flamboyant set of *Variations brillantes* on airs from Hérold's opera *Pré aux Clercs*. The latter, but the first of several such effusions (always 'brillantes'), shows extraordinary control of the piano but musically is of no interest. The Sonata, however, is different because it shows the usual affinity with its models and is absolutely sure as regards form.

Written in two parts, it is slender in material. It is very close to those early works of Beethoven, which were written when he was eleven for his patron, and in some respects almost superior. It might be called 'pastiche à la Mozart'. The most notable point about it is its tentative feeling for extraneous keys although the general key successions are strictly to letter. The following example is more than a boyish awkwardness. So far as Franck's future is concerned, it may well be regarded as a presage.

Ex. 122

The *Deuxième Grande Sonate* need detain us no longer than to remark that it contains a hint at the cyclic form in an embryo state which may have been accidental.

It is not till 1842 that we find the first published piece for piano, an *Eclogue* which, although opening in a square manner, contains the following example of pianism which can be ascribed solely to Franck's large hands and his occupation with that virtuosic music which his musicianship carried a little further than mere display.

Ex. 123

It looks complicated in this form, and Vincent d'Indy points out that had Franck been established, his publisher would have allowed three staves, which makes the whole thing easy.

The future *Fantaisies* on national and operatic airs are exactly what might be expected of them and it is better to pass them by. So far as the *Variations brillantes* go, they contain the germs of the future and although they are musically devoid of any interest whatsoever, they served as good training grounds for the *Variations symphoniques* and the adoption of the variation in the cyclic form.

I can find no trace of the *Duo on God Save the King*, and a *Fantaisie* for piano dated 1844 in the list is presumed to have been planned for a publisher but never written.

Looking at these early published works and the earlier MSS one can see frequently how the musicianship in Franck came to the fore over and above the technical display for which they were composed. The MSS contain more promise than the published works because he was allowed to write what he wanted without father standing behind him. No doubt father regarded them as mere boyish attempts and as long as the piano itself was practised, he did not mind what happened in between times. The published music shows the insistence of father on everything the young man did.

A few short pieces were written for certain little pupils between 1846 and 1873. In the latter year he produced a version
of the *Prélude, Fugue, et Variation* for piano and harmonium, the
piano part being a slightly elaborated arrangement of the left
hand of the organ work—the harmonium plays the melody. The
piano was used again in 1879 in the Quintet and in 1884 for *Les
Djinns*; but this year saw the composition of one of his best
loved works, the *Prélude, Choral, et Fugue*.

There are certain works in a medium which time has proved
to be outstanding not only for loftiness of conception but for
clearly marked enterprise and originality. Such works are the
'Hammerklavier' and Op. 111 Sonatas of Beethoven. The
Brahms-Handel variations come under the same heading. In
between times can be placed the *Prélude, Choral, et Fugue* of
Franck. Always remembering the period of which we are speaking, Franck used almost the entire resources of the piano in this
work. He used it lyrically, chordally, and contrapuntally. The
bravura writing continues the line of the Beethoven concertos
and whenever there is padding, it is always thematic. He proved
his mastery of variation since the entire work is based upon a
germ from which the music grows.

His original plan was to write a Prelude and Fugue which
might be a worthy opposite number to the '48'. The idea of the
Choral grew during the course of the composing process when
he felt that the two movements required some kind of a link; but
in the first place it was never intended that this link should be of
any length or significance. What the work lacked in its original
planning was something 'cantabile', some sustained melody
which would relieve the onward rush of the Prelude. From this
link sprung the whole Choral and its subsequent use in the
Fugue.

The spirit of the Prelude, however, is much more that of some
of the organ Preludes of Bach than of the '48'. Franck loved the
rolling effect of the diapasons, the dignity of the Toccata in F,
for example, but fortunately he did not attempt to use organ
technique. What his opinion was of such massacres as Tausig
and Liszt carried out on the organ works of Bach would be
enlightening to read. Organists as a race either despise them or
laugh at them. Franck kept the fact that he was writing

piano music in mind and avoided the pitfalls of an organ background.

The Prelude opens with an immediate reference to the germ which is hidden in the arpeggio writing.

Ex. 124

This germ becomes significant at the eighth bar and after this appearance completely governs the thought.

Ex. 125

It is suggested earlier, in the fifth bar, when an upward surge in the left hand puts us in mind of a moment in the third Choral for organ.

Ex. 126

An interesting variation of it comes in the interludial passage between the first and second bravura passages.

Ex. 127

Great importance must be placed on this fragment as we shall find it used in the Choral.

Ex. 125 returns in the key of F sharp minor and is considerably extended. An echo of the first Trio and an anticipation of the 'Finale' of the next large piano work may be seen in this passage, which may be said to invert the germ figure.

Ex. 128

The Prelude carries on with its opening cadenza-like writing and leads direct into the Choral. The Choral theme, however, does not enter at once. The whole of this section is built on the principle of theme and interlude. The interludial matter is one of those infinite themes which seem Heaven-sent. It is quoted almost in full in Chapter Four. Suffice it here to remark how Ex. 127 becomes an integral part of it.

Ex. 129

The Choral theme is anticipatory of the slow movement of the Symphony where the repeated note at 'A' bears a clear family likeness to the second half of the Symphony theme.

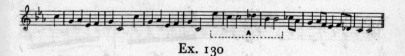

Ex. 130

At the close of the Choral where, incidentally, editions vary as to F and F flat at the final cadence (the original F flat is

147

perfectly logical) there is another interlude which announces the subject of the fugue in a harmonic form. This is continued for thirty bars of writing which is sheer thematic pianism. In these few bars can be found the whole matter of the Fugue. A sweeping little figure reminds us of the Symphony—this constant anticipation of a later work makes us suspect that Franck had the idea in his mind when writing this piano work.

Ex. 131

The Fugue overlaps this section. It is always satisfactory to the player, but Saint-Saëns, who played it at its first performance, thought little of it and remarked that it soon stopped being a fugue. What he meant was that the writing is not consistently contrapuntal. On the second page, for example, the subject appears underneath 'chop-stick' chords and later there is some arpeggio writing which in academic groves is not considered good fugal technique.

The subject itself has grown out of the Prelude and Choral.

Ex. 132

It is treated by inversion, augmentation and diminution, and there are the usual stretti. At the climax, Franck suggests a return to the Prelude which is followed by an appearance of the Choral in the simplest decorated form. The pianism rests but for a short while, and then this subject and that of the Fugue are combined in a manner which is masterly not only thematically but in the way it avoids the obvious.

Ex. 133

Like so many of Franck's works the weak moment is the coda. There are some themes which simply will not stand change of mode. The theme of the Choral is one of them and the closing bars are cheap and vulgar to our ears, although in their time were the customary manner of ending a work and one which had not then grown threadbare. We hesitate to quote this one blot:

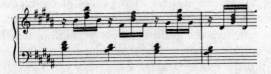

Ex. 134

The *Prélude, Choral, et Fugue* says everything which Bach would have said had he had the piano of Franck's time. It says everything that Liszt, Tausig, and Busoni tried to make Bach say. It is not only virtuoso music for the virtuoso player; it is magnificent music *per se*. It offers little openings for 'interpretation', but gives the player every opportunity for his technique, and he requires a brain as well as finger dexterity. The purist likes to regard it as a 'Prelude, Choral, and Fugato' because the fugue does not conform to the basic text book idea of what such a thing should be. Apart from the semitonal left hand octaves in the Prelude, it is singularly free from the Franck chromaticism which some find so oppressive. The one element which it avoids is the cantabile melody. The themes do not sing as much as they progress, for their basis is mainly chordal and when there is arpeggio or figured accompaniment to them, there is invariably a chordal underlay in the right hand.

Harmonically it is one of the clearest of Franck's major works. Its chromatic range is limited and it is easier to describe it as being 'in a key' than the Symphony, for example. The innovations of yesterday become, of course, the conventions of today, hence what appear to us to be very ordinary arpeggio 'fill-ups', were once recognized as being perfectly legitimate and had not had time to become conventional. The really conventional writing in this work is found at the first appearance of the Choral theme in the Fugue and the final cadence. Otherwise the spread of the arpeggio writing is individually Franck.

The *Prélude, Aria, et Final* is the direct opposite of the *Prélude, Choral, et Fugue*. The writing throughout is mainly chordal and there is no pianism worth mentioning until the last movement. The player plunges straight into the opening theme without any preparation and the work does not start so much as begin. It is virtually a sonata in three movements. The cyclic form is used with such complete mastery that points of contact are found everywhere and it is sometimes difficult to distinguish between those places where the quotations are textually intentional and those where they are merely figuration and, therefore, fortuitous. With all this the work hangs well together.

The chordal nature of the writing once more offers opportunities for those who cry 'the organ again', because there are certain features about it which undoubtedly find their origin in pedal passages with sustained manual harmonies, and left hand tenths with the lower third, easy if the pedal plays the lowest note but devilish awkward for the ordinary hand. There is, however, no other work which is written on quite the same lines. The chromaticism is consistent and the music ranges through practically every key. Of ingenuity there is an abundance yet we are not all the time conscious of it and some of the permutations become apparent only after repeated hearings or close examination.

The first movement is in three clearly defined sections, the first two coming to a deliberate halt. The third goes on to the end, and in it the material is welded together rather than extended. The material is both thematic in itself, and accompanimental. Wherever one looks one sees derivations from this or that fragment and the whole process is perfectly natural and musical.

The main theme is as follows:

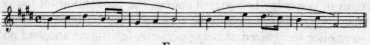

Ex. 135

This governs the whole work but is not used in any fragmentary manner nor is it the basis of any fresh material.

The second theme which opens the second whole section is as serene as the first is dignified.

Ex. 136

The second half is derived from a fragment in the first section which accompanies the principal subject when it appears in the left hand.

Ex. 137 'A' and 'B'

It is when we come to the third section that the interest in construction begins. This subject is in two distinct parts.

Ex. 138 'A' and 'B'

'B' acquires a thematic significance and within its limited compass accomplishes a good deal.

Ex. 139

Later it becomes the accompaniment to the theme in the right hand in diminution with its original appearance.

Ex. 140

A subsidiary theme in descending thirds derives from a figure which appears in the first section. It is of considerable importance in the third movement.

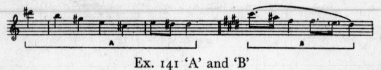

Ex. 141 'A' and 'B'

Particularly interesting is the use both in its original shape and by inversion of a small figure which as the work progresses assumes increasing importance, to acquire thematic rank in the coda.

Ex. 142

The form of the movement is difficult to determine. M Alfred Cortot in his *French Piano Music* refers to the first section as the Exposition and to the second as the Second Subject, but there are two clearly defined themes in the first section, of which the second reminds us slightly of a Gregorian intonation.

Ex. 143

What can be said, therefore, of the third section which opens with new material and does nothing to extend what we have already heard except to play with it in the above-mentioned manner? It approximates by reason of the constant appearance of the principal subject to Old Rondo form, but since the music of the episodes appears continually in some form or other, such a description is a little free. Probably it would be nearer the mark to call it a Free Fantasia, and let it be realized at once that there is nothing improvisatory about it. The main subject comes in three times in the first section, once in the second, and four times in the third in varying keys and moods. It is in turn quiet and dignified, martial and strident, playful, triumphant, and finally serene. Commencing in E major, it eventually finds itself in A flat minor, moving homewards by means of a convenient enharmonic change, but passing through F major before making the final tonic conclusion, the movement finishing with Ex. 143.

The Aria is one of Franck's loveliest movements. It is closely packed and finely wrought. Once it has got under way there seems hardly a progression which cannot be justified thematically by some previous entry. The introduction does not merely introduce the main theme and then merge into it; it becomes of significance in the last movement, and even a contrapuntal episode linking one part of the subject to another is revealed as in double counterpoint. Further an ordinary rise in the treble of the dominant to the tonic on the dominant seventh chord which resolves straight into the main theme has its own importance in the closing coda of the work.

There is nothing venturesome in the pianism of the introduction, but the descending fourths are of importance.

Ex. 144

The main theme is in three sections, each of which is repeated in the lower register after appearing in the higher. It is a complete sixteen bar sentence with 'interruptions'. The entire theme is as follows:

Ex. 145

153

The little figure quoted in Ex. 142 forms a link, in the first place, between the second and third parts of the theme and later on becomes the material of an episode, and later on still, is inverted.

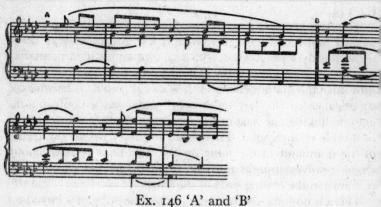

Ex. 146 'A' and 'B'

The movement ends with a coda built on the descending fourth figure of the introduction.

Even when part of the theme is used in the bass it is always in the nature of a counter-subject and not just as a bass.

In form it is simple ternary with short episode, the length of the subject being in itself sufficient to make the movement satisfactory.

The Final gives us some rhythmic pianism. The theme is derived entirely from Ex. 141 'A'. This is treated at some length when the second subject makes its appearance preceded by a link based on Ex. 145 'A'. This second subject is very vulgar and commonplace. While it has considerable verve and triumph there is no gainsaying its 'earthiness'.

Ex. 147

After a restatement of the opening theme, the principal subject of the Aria (Ex. 145 parts 1 and 2) is introduced as an episode, being treated in diminution also. A recurrence of Ex. 147 in E major leads to Ex. 135, the main theme of the whole work, in strong minim chords over a quaver octave bass. In the left hand there is a quaint reference to the Choral from the previous piano work which seems to escape most commentators, but this must not be taken as another symptom of cyclicism.

The coda is interesting as not only do we have a reference to the third part of Ex. 145 but even the fragment at Ex. 142 is used, and the work ends as quietly as it began with the opening theme of the Aria, in minims.

If we take this work as music first of all, it is magnificent, the least satisfactory of the three movements being the first because of its cloying chromaticism. Viewed architecturally it is a monument of resource. Those who view piano music in the light of pianism find next to nothing here, and it is significant that a consensus of opinion amongst composers has revealed that they consider it the better of the two works, while pianists hold the other opinion.

These two works Franck wrote with a view to making the piano an important factor in musical expression, in the same way that Ravel, many years later, wrote *Gaspard de la Nuit*. Both the Franck works are abstract music even though there is a romantic feeling in the second. The qualification is necessary because of the theory today that abstract music must be cold and calculating. The feeling in the first is not of this earth. It is spiritual and lacks the humanities of the second. The two sides of Franck's character are admirably illustrated in these works.

Chapter Nine

The Choral Works

WITH the choral works we find ourselves faced with the worst music Franck ever wrote, culminating with some of his best. By the same token this assessment includes his church music, which is even more insignificant. Nevertheless, it is important to remember the period of the works in question, and what immediately preceded them. The composers for whom Franck had the greatest admiration included Méhul, whose memory is kept fairly green by his opera *Joseph*. In the world of oratorio there was no tradition in France to work upon. The oratorios of Handel were not widely known and the Passions and Masses of Bach sealed books save to those fortunate ones who had come across them, often by chance. Reicha, we have already seen, was one of the few who took the trouble to inquire into them, and Boëly, the organist of St Germain l'Auxerrois, played the available organ works and communicated their value to Franck. The motets were completely unknown and Bach himself was considered by the unthinking few who knew of him as just another organist.

There was, therefore, no choral tradition in France and choral music was viewed entirely from the angle of four-part vocal harmony exercises. His own choral writing would seem to have been the result of complete inexperience and this general blot does not appear to have been eradicated as his life advanced. Many of the errors of judgment in the early works were repeated in *Les Béatitudes*, by which time he might reasonably have been expected to have learnt a few things; but the contrapuntists did not come his way, and it may well be wondered why his natural instrumental fluency in counterpoint should not have been applied to other fields.

It is in this respect, but in this respect only, that the choral works of Gounod are superior to those of Franck, for the former at least used the voices with independent freedom.

The first of the oratorios, described as a 'Biblical Eclogue' was *Ruth*, a simple-minded effusion which binds all the weaknesses of the period in one cover. Although *Ruth* is absolutely unperformable today, it cannot be written off by the student of Franck, because it contains a good many of the future Franckian characteristics, is written in the best of taste, and is a pointer to the prevailing conditions of its time. It could not be performed today with any seriousness because it is too clearly naïve and mid-Victorian. Yet certain movements, particularly the solo and duet ones, are not without merit. There is always a flowing vocal line and now and again the ear is struck with sudden key changes, too abrupt to be modulations, which foretold the future and which must have struck the contemporary ears with some force. The copy in front of me bears the inscription in Franck's handwriting 'à mon élève et ami, John Hinton'. The copy evidently was used for some performance, because there are some percussion cues marked in pencil, not in Franck's writing, and a few indications of horn entries; further, there are some exclamations such as 'Good' pencilled-in at odd places. Significantly enough these exclamations appear invariably at some startling key change, particularly at a direct move from the common chord of G to F sharp. There are also a few corrections written by Franck himself. Whether this performance was one unrecorded in England or not cannot be ascertained.

This same copy, incidentally, is bound up with Mendelssohn's *Athalie*. Close examination shows that there is almost nothing to choose between the works save that the Priests of Mendelssohn march with greater vigour than the Israelites of Franck and the choral writing of the former is the more independent of the two. This comparison goes to show that Franck was not the only composer writing indifferent music in Europe at the time.

A good point may be found in the March of the Israelites, which has a certain dignity.

Ex. 148

The vocal lines are all graceful and singable. Vincent d'Indy draws attention to the similarity of one to an aria from Massenet's *Manon*, but this must have been quite coincidental. The duet between Ruth and Boaz (the French version of this name is, unfortunately, 'Booz') is very graceful and the whole thing completely unassuming. The description of the work as an 'Eclogue' explains its simplicity and its fresh pastoral movements are quite convincing if a mental sound picture of the orchestra is maintained.

The choral writing is square and uninteresting. Sentences are repeated over and over again with nothing in view except to make the choral movements last longer. The orchestration is quite colourful and effective and what on paper in the piano arrangement sounds altogether too artless, comes off in full performance. Its merits, therefore, are almost negative ones, its demerits positive—but it is music of the period and in its proper background, undoubtedly well up to the standard, even though that standard may not have been a very high one. It is the music of a young man of the time, his first serious extended work. We may agree that too much was expected of it at its first performance and too much ascribed to it at its second.

The next choral work, *La Tour de Babel*, though unpublished, is a great advance on *Ruth*. Franck chose Latin words and these seem to have loosened a good deal of his density of choral thought. The MS, written as usual in impeccable writing, shows the care and thought bestowed upon it, and although it is by no means as facile as *Ruth*, it has no signs of being laboured. Why Franck forbade publication is difficult to see in view of what he allowed to be printed. It is certainly different from the works which we shall consider, but this does not make it of inferior quality. Even in 1865 Franck showed his inability to be really violent and the choice of subject called for the viciousness of a

Berlioz to make it convincing; this, however, does not explain the veto on publication because he himself was quite incapable of realizing his limitations.

The opening theme on the strings, 'martellato', has vigour, but no strength because of its limited range.

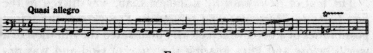

Ex. 149

The subject does not deal with the erection of the tower and its subsequent results in the way that Berlioz would have treated it, but is concerned solely with the voices of the humans and of God.

An interesting point about the work is the fugue to the words 'Celebremur nomen nostrum',

Ex. 150

because although he had fugue 'at his finger tips' so to speak, he wrote so few of them; the *Prélude, Fugue, et Variation*, *Prélude, Choral, et Fugue*, one section of the second *Choral* and certain sections of *Les Béatitudes* are the only ones we can find which completely satisfy as complete entities in the form.

The contrapuntal element in this work was repeated in two choruses, also unpublished, *La Plainte des Israélites* and *Le Cantique de Moïse*—Vincent d'Indy does not mention these works. They are also set to Latin words. The former is interesting because Franck establishes his chromaticism in a passage such as this:

Ex. 151

The writing in both these short works is contrapuntally superior even to *La Tour de Babel*. For what purpose they were written and what was the impulse are unknown. They were never performed and may be regarded as exercises towards *Les Béatitudes*.

The text of *Rédemption* by Edouard Blau, was offered in the first place to Massenet, who refused it. Franck saw the latent possibilities of a book which clearly delineated the situation of a world before and after hearing the voice of God and was immediately drawn towards it in the way that the theatre-loving Massenet could never have been. The text is not the least theatrical in the way that *Marie Madeleine* offered such treatment and Massenet was not of the ilk to propound ideals.

Rédemption is the first of Franck's really important choral works, and in many ways it is a failure. In the first place the choral writing is once more too chordal and there is none of the contrapuntal writing of *La Tour de Babel*. In the second place all the vices of the period are found in its pages, particularly the habit of reiterating chords either in triplets or even-quavers. Here we do find a spirituality but the symphonic interlude where it is most marked is mawkish and sentimental.

The work is in three parts, with a short orchestral introduction. Part One describes the situation on earth before the dawn of Christ. Man seeks to find happiness in pleasure and hatred which can result only in death. A flight of angels announces the birth of Christ and the redemption of the world.

The Introduction is slow moving music of an amorphous character. It neither sets the scene nor prophesies the future. It is music of a high nature and impulse and is contrapuntal throughout in spite of the rather static quality of its leading theme.

Ex. 152

Photo PIERRE PETIT

1870

Guy Ropartz

Pierre de Bréville

Vincent d'Indy

Students of canon can find an excellent lesson here in the orchestral web.

Part One opens with a chorus depicting the outlook of humanity in its degenerate days. It is not satisfactory. If humanity was no more evil than this, then there was not very much wrong, but here we must emphasize that in each of the three big choral works Franck concentrated on letting the words express themselves. The evil they implied needed no implementation on the part of the music and it is in this principle that both his failure and success lie. He fails because the resultant music does not convince the listener, since it does not match up with the spirit of the text. He succeeds only with those who believe in letting the words express themselves. The weakness of the choral writing lies in its squareness and block harmony which moves over a constant reiteration of chords in 6/8 time. It is tedious because it lacks anything compelling.

It is followed by a long spoken passage which explains and laments the present with a premonition of the future. The spoken voice eventually has a musical background, and the chorus of Angels, built upon Ex. 162, carries the story onwards. The three part writing here is better, although still square. When it changes into two parts we get some excellent imitations, but the general impression is sentimental rather than seraphic. A long and quite dramatic recitative and aria for the Archangel is interspersed with orchestral music which foreshadows the Symphonic Interlude to follow.

The final chorus, in E major, is spoilt by the constant repetition of the chordal accompaniment. The choral writing does not differ in quality from anything as yet heard, but here it seems more in place. The salute to the Babe in the Cradle, however, is a little too forceful and triumphant, and in this we have an interesting contrast to the idea of Berlioz in *L'Enfance de Christ*, and, of course, the cradle song in the *Christmas Oratorio*.

Now follows the Symphonic Interlude, which is quite different from that originally composed. Franck attempted to depict the passage of centuries. Persecution has been in vain. Belief has vanished to give place to a return to the pagan habits of life. This music is beautiful until it tries to become horrible. The original interlude, still in MS, shows that the basic idea was just the same and failed just where this one fails. Both have their dramatic moments which read like indifferent Liszt. As long as one does not know that these moments are what they are intended to be, there is a nobility about them which is quite compelling, but putting their intention against the notes, they fail because, in exactly the same way that the world at the beginning of the work did not seem a bad place, so humanity does not seem to be very noticeably evil.

The only attempts at delineation are the harp passages which at that period, and for some time after, appear to have been the standard method of delineating angels and Heavenly Hosts.

Mankind is filled with horror. Everything is dark, and 'the earth is accursed'. The opening theme is not unrelated to Ex. 149 from *La Tour de Babel* which proves that the aforesaid tower was also not as bad as it was painted:

Ex. 153

The music is emphatic and reasonably awesome, but one thinks of the Darkness chorus in *Israel in Egypt* and sees why this purposely un-underlined music fails to convince. Only a great poem can succeed in these circumstances, and Edouard Blau was not a great poet.

Another long spoken passage follows, again with a musical background in its later stages, and then the angels lament the state of things. They veil their faces in sorrow. The Archangel sings of the new redemption—in music of such a jejune and simple nature as to be hardly credible. Here Franck unconsciously writes an aria akin to those simple moments in the operas of Adolphe Adam. It wakes up at the words 'But when this God calls him to hold him in His arms, rebellious man does not obey', but gets into the same rut as Spohr's *Last Judgement* without that work's chromaticism.

A spoken passage tells that redemption may come through prayer, penitence, and a recognition of brotherly love among mankind. The final chorus in which the writing is considerably freer for the voices declaims man's intention to find redemption in that manner. This is effective and not unimpressive in its Gallic manner, the manner, it must be repeated, of its period. Here we can see the fundamental difference between Franck and Gounod when dealing with such a subject. In spite of the musical weaknesses of Franck's music, it is deeply sincere and genuinely felt. No doubt Gounod would say that he was equally sincere and felt as deeply, but there is that ring about *Rédemption* which is lacking in Gounod. Franck, we know, really did practise the tenets of brotherly love. Gounod may have thought he did, but there are instances of his acting otherwise, having a spiteful tongue.

We are faced with another work which it would be bad policy to perform today because it is not near enough to our own time nor high enough to rank as a standard work. Its main virtue is its sincerity, its chief faults those conventions of its period which date it.

The original version of *Rédemption* was composed in 1871 and was written in six months. The second in which he wrote a new Interlude and added the final chorus for men, was done in 1874. He had started *Les Béatitudes* in 1869. Vincent d'Indy tells that after the first rehearsal of *Rédemption* the orchestral parts were so full of mistakes that he, Duparc, and Benoist sat up all night correcting them, d'Indy feeling that, as a result, if all else failed, he would at least be able to earn a living as a copyist.

Les Béatitudes was constantly interrupted during its progress and was not finished until 1879, the intervening ten years seeing the composition of *Les Éolides*, the *Trois Pièces pour Grand Orgue*, and the Piano Quintet. Also there was the song *Paris* which he wrote literally in one breath during a bombardment of the city.

Whatever may have been the faults of the previous works, if they are repeated in *Les Béatitudes*, they are more than compensated for by the good points of the work. H. C. Colles in Vol. VII of *The Oxford History of Music* compares it with the Brahms Requiem in that the two works are the biggest of their period and show the divergence of approach between the Teutonic and Gallic minds. Brahms always underlines the text by the curve of the music and the two are closely knit. Franck, as usual, let the words express themselves and hangs the music upon them.

Franck delayed the composition of *Les Béatitudes* for so many years owing to the difficulty of finding a suitable poet for the text. Although there were a large number of hack librettists available, he hesitated at employing them. At long last the wife of one of the professors at the Lycée, Mme Colomb, undertook the task and although she was not a good poet, her text was at least adequate. In 1869 Franck started the music.

Having formulated the intention at the beginning of his career and thought about it constantly, he had a pretty good idea of the plan and how he would set it. Thus the Prologue presented no difficulties.

The work treats each Beatitude separately, preceded by an exposition of the conditions of the world as regards the beatific message. Then follows a middle section which deals with the regeneration, and the conclusion is the voice of Christ delivering the message itself. Each part, therefore, is in complete ternary form as regards its literary basis. The Prologue sets the picture of the conditions which the librettist imagined as prevalent at the time of the Sermon on the Mount, although the circumstances are equally applicable to many periods in world history.

'At this time there was so much misery on the earth that not a single heart had any hope. . . . One voice was heard, as soft as honey, and the disinherited, forgetting their sorrow, raised their eyes to Heaven.' In simple music mainly for Tenor solo Franck introduces the first words. There is no attempt to paint any picture. The music is a bare statement of the facts.

The opening theme is not exactly the same as a Wagnerian leitmotiv, but it governs the entire thought.

Ex. 154

It has been argued that the whole of this Prologue is too warm for the spirit of the words, and this charge is not without some justification; but the basis is the idea of redemption and regeneration and Franck was perfectly right in presenting the two differing ideas of the music and the text. The guiding theme gives a feeling of melancholy if not of sadness.

The first Beatitude—'Blessed are the poor in spirit'—begins

very unsatisfactorily and is the weakest movement in the whole
work. Apart from the fact that it repeats the words unneces-
sarily—'Let us follow riches with ardour'—the writing for tenors
and basses is mostly in thirds and octaves. When it breaks into
four parts things get a little better, but up to that point it is dull.
The tonality does not go very far from the key of A minor and
considerable use is made of the chord of the diminished seventh.
The music becomes less stiff when it changes to F sharp minor;
from this point the interest and æsthetic appeal increase and it
is as if Franck had at last got into his stride; but the opening
subject returns in due course, becoming wearisome to the ear
simply because the text did not inspire the composer and does
not do so to the listener.

When the voice of Christ enters Franck adopts his favourite
key of F sharp. He had a predilection for it all through his life.
(It is said that Saint-Saëns took strong exception to its use by
Debussy in *Printemps*, remarking that 'one does not write for
orchestra in the key of F sharp'.) The music is reflective of the
Prologue, especially noteworthy being the descent in thirds.

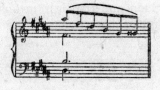

Ex. 155

A short rhythmic figure plays an important part later in the
work, which is thus well knit in the cyclic manner.

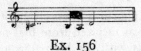

Ex. 156

The celestial choir closes the movement with some lovely
music. Here there is plenty of canonic writing, mainly at the
octave, while the orchestra plays a passage in descending thirds
through the compass of two octaves.

Franck does not make any attempt to write pictorially celestial music here. We think of other 'celestial choirs'—Elgar's in *Gerontius*, Vaughan Williams's in *The Shepherds of the Delectable Mountains*; the first with its spread harp chords and ejaculations of the word 'Praise'; the second repetitive on a figure rather than a theme. We can forgive all the weakness and squareness of the opening of this movement for the exquisite close.

The faithful Vincent d'Indy is under no illusions as to the opening section, likening it to the vulgar operatic melodies of Meyerbeer—indeed, he even refers to the 'Judaic' period of opera by which we know that his dislike was racial at root. The fact is that Franck had singularly little self-criticism in his make-up and when a particular section of the text did not interest him or lay outside his natural expression, he was content with almost the first thought which came to him, although this movement gave him considerable trouble.

The second Beatitude (the order is not that of the authorized version)—'Blessed are the meek'—opens with an orchestral prelude and is immediately followed by a choral fugue which is beautifully proportioned. It is noble music. Franck here does paint a picture of gloom and despair by means of a subject which has little line and is cleanly sectional.

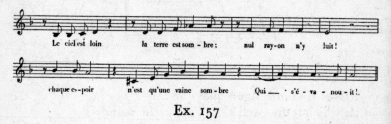

Ex. 157

The whole of this chorus is intensely emotional and fully contrapuntal. Franck was inspired from first note to last here and the movement ranks with the highest achievements in music. The concluding voice of Christ gains accordingly by its simplicity. This is one of the shortest of the movements and there is not a single note or passage too many.

The third —'Blessed are they who mourn'—has a solemn tread-like ground in the orchestra, the chorus singing a broad

theme in unison, in conception not unlike the second chorus of
the Brahms Requiem. The dropping third in the orchestral part
characterizes a great part of the musical thought.

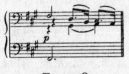

Ex. 158

Here the squareness of the choral writing is most suitable, as
it portrays the inexorable tread of hopelessness and frustration.

The text then introduces a personal note in the form of a wife,
a husband, an orphan, a mother, and a chorus of slaves. The
depth of despond is reached. The slaves have rather an ordinary
tune which resembles the theme of the first movement of the
Symphony and Franck uses it also for a chorus of philosophers.
In spite of its approaching banality (although that is perhaps
too strong a word) the mood never alters and in the same way
that the voice of Christ simplified the stress of the second Beatitude, so, here, the voice, with its pure and diatonic line, brings
its message of hope and comfort.

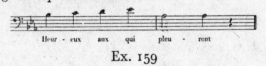

Heur - eux aux qui pleu - rent

Ex. 159

The succeeding celestial chorus enlarges upon it.

Particularly impressive is the orchestral prelude to the fourth
Beatitude—'Blessed are they who hunger and thirst after
righteousness'. Here a new theme is introduced which d'Indy
calls the 'element of desire'.

Ex. 160

This has more curve than anything so far heard and is indeed
truly Franckian. It is followed by a theme of hope and confidence.

167

Ex. 161

Its ki nship with the second subject of the Symphony is obvious
at once, and may account for Harvey Grace's appellation of
this second subject as the 'motive of Faith' in his article in
Grove's Dictionary, although originally this description was given
to the subject of the second movement.

The prelude leads straight into a long tenor solo which is
marred by the repeated chordal accompaniment, which we have
found to have been a characteristic of the period and 'the way
they did things' in those days. There is no chorus and the voice
of Christ delivers its message over Ex. 161 and subsequently
Ex. 159.

Beatitude five—'Blessed are the merciful'—at once introduces
the device of inversion, for it opens with the inverted form of
Ex. 154.

Ex. 162

After a short tenor solo there is a chorus of considerable power
which just fails to convince. Franck's inability to delineate
violence is very clearly shown here and although we would not
go so far as to agree with d'Indy's description of it as smacking
of the theatre of Meyerbeer, we must agree that it is not up to
the standard of the preceding movements. On the other hand it
is much less banal and much more dramatic than the first
Beatitude. There is really no possible objection to be taken to a
dramatic chorus in an oratorio whether the words be scriptural
invective or poet's feeling. Mendelssohn failed lamentably in
this respect in the Baal choruses in *Elijah*, Elgar in the orgy scene
in *The Apostles*, and both tried to be dramatic. No objection has
been taken to the inclusion of these two attempts and there is
nothing valid in the case of Franck; but Vincent d'Indy would
have us in a state of incense and genuflection throughout.

Looking at it dispassionately, one can see little theatrical influence in this movement, but can deplore the square choral writing.

As in the case of the first movement, the weaknesses are atoned for by the concluding section, where the voice of Christ and the celestial choir, together with the Angel of Pardon, combine in music so beautiful that it really does not seem of this earth.

The next movement—'Blessed are the pure in heart'—is interesting for a chorus of Jewish and Hebrew women regretting their old gods which have fallen into disuse. The teaching of Reicha is evident here in the use of the polymodality of B flat minor and D flat major which combine without any effort.

A conversation between the Pharisees is emphatic and perhaps over-dramatized, but a passage like this at first sight makes us think of J. S. Bach.

Ex. 163

The final section is very extended and developed and is almost as long as the first two put together, but it is lovely music and Franck reveals a true part of himself.

'Blessed are the peacemakers'—the seventh Beatitude—opens ominously on the orchestra and the air is full of threats, but, alas, we descend into the depths of what with another composer would be banality but, knowing Franck and his music, is more humorous than pathetic. Franck's adventures with Evil and its personifications of Satan were never happy. The prelude leads into a long solo for Satan which is far from being satanic and the subsequent chorus of tyrants is truly commonplace. It is difficult to reconcile oneself to the frenzied shouting of the crowd in an amiable 6/8 time, but eventually the music does rise above all this and Satan's ejaculations interspersed with chorus almost convince us, but only because by that time we have become acclimatized to the general thought.

It is impossible to put any of the blame on to the text here for it is actually rather suggestive. The moment when the voice of Christ proclaims the words and Satan owns to defeat is very genuine and impressive within its small compass. The movement ends with an extended ensemble for the five soloists and such is the balance that there is no suggestion of overweight anywhere. Once more the accompaniment descends to the repeated chord technique.

The eighth Beatitude—'Blessed are they who are persecuted for righteousness' sake'—crowns the work with glory. A twelve bar prelude leads straight into Satan once more, and here the writing and treatment are above reproach. Satan is no longer a demoniacal force but becomes a conquered king who refuses to accept defeat. He declaims his music over an accompaniment largely consisting of the theme of Beatitude seven. His reply to a quiet chorus of the righteous is dramatic without being melo-dramatic. In vain he defies the world. A very moving chorus follows—'O Eternal Righteousness'—in which Franck's imagination had full play. The Mater Dolorosa has a long and effective solo and Satan, this time in terror, breaks in under celestial music represented by very ordinary harp arpeggii (but, be it emphasized once more, very much of their period). A duet between the voice of Christ and Satan is very well contrasted by means of simple chord successions in the case of the former and four bars of emphatic writing in the latter. At the words of Satan 'My kingdom is conquered' the voice of Christ in triumph (and fortissimo for the first time) exclaims 'Come, O blessed of my Father' and the work ends with the Hosannas of the Celestial choir.

The weaknesses of the work cannot be denied. Its frequent banality, its dull patches, its lack of power in its violent moments, all these must be admitted by its admirers. Its lack of spirituality is sometimes reckoned as a matter for blame, but this very lack serves as an answer to those who always speak deprecatingly of Franck's alleged 'spirituality'. Its very directness refutes this charge for surely this subject itself would have been the very one for such expression. It is, as Duparc said, 'simply music'. It is very beautiful (and that cannot be denied) and beautiful without being heavy.

In this respect we can turn to Elgar's *The Apostles* and note how different the approach was at those moments when the Beatitudes appear. We can also note the close similarity to Ex. 161 of the theme which Elgar uses so frequently during the work. The only difference, as Mr Cecil Gray says in his *A Survey of Contemporary Music*, is that one is in quadruple time and the other in triple. We mention this only as a coincidence which is all the more interesting because the subjects of the two works are interlocked in certain degrees.

Les Béatitudes bridges the gap from Beethoven's Mass in D. It is not as great as that work, but it is not derogatory to Franck or to any other composer to say that he was not as great as Beethoven.

Les Béatitudes is a work big in concept but never portentous. It will never be really popular with choral societies because it lacks the wide sweeps of vocal line which singers love to sing. Nevertheless, it is certainly more than musicians' music and its deep sincerity is moving. We think of that first private performance with a chorus of twenty and piano accompaniment....

Franck wrote one more choral work, *Rébecca*, which he wrote for The Amateur Choral Society and its founder, Antonin Guillot de Sainbris, in 1881. It appears to be unprocurable now for stock, but an examination of the copy in the Conservatoire Library shows it to have been an advance on Franck's usual outlook on choral writing. The voice parts are treated with more line and interdependence, but the orchestra plays a very subordinate part—not that it is an unobtrusive background but for once the voices are allowed to justify the work as a choral one. Performances have been impossible to trace other than one by the Schola Cantorum on 16th May 1911 at the Salle Gaveau. It is in the line of the two short choruses which were never published or performed.

Chapter Ten

The Operas

FRANCK was attracted to opera at an early age. His early essay in the genre, *Le Valet de Ferme*, he did not allow to be published, firstly because he knew the music to be inferior and secondly because it was his first disappointment and he never liked to refer to it. We cannot dwell on it, therefore. However, there has come to light in the Bibliothéque nationale in Paris a MS for voice and piano of an opera *Stradella* of which no mention is made by Vincent d'Indy. The MS is undated but the first page holds the signature of the early works, 'César Auguste Franck de Liége' and the Lyre with the initials 'C.A.F.'. We can reasonably date it from the early days. The music is more mature and individual than the Trios but exactly why it got no further than this stage cannot be stated. Inside the MS there is a sheet of paper giving a list of certain arias, etc., which can or may have been performed with piano at some time. It is a cheerful little work with a spirited introduction. The texture would suggest 'Opéra-Comique'. A comparison with *Le Valet de Ferme* would be interesting, but this work is not available. Why d'Indy and Maurice Emmanuel made no mention of it is impossible to say and Franck seems to have been reticent about it. There is no full score as far as can be found. Perhaps Franck wrote it for practice, although it is very much more than a mere exercise. The subject was treated by Niedermeyer and Flotow as well, and first conjecture led to the possibility of Franck's having copied one of them, as students do. Comparison, however, shows that this is not so, and the work in question is quite original.

The two published operas, *Hulda* and *Ghisèle*, made no impression on their production. This is both easy to see and difficult to understand. It is easy to see that the music although strong lacks that theatrical tang which is essential to opera. The music is, actually, too good for its purpose but it is never dull; it simply does not fit into the general idea of what operatic music should be. It is difficult to understand why only certain isolated movements from *Hulda* should have survived. These, the 'March and Ballet Music', are the weakest movements in the work from the musical standard, because their *raison d'être* made them of a type and pattern which did not require much thought. Certain arias and other instrumental movements, however, are well worthy of performance. Another obstacle to their production is that one does not associate Franck with the theatre and no matter how one regards him, it is as a symphonic and organ composer that his reputation remains.

In the same way that Franck let his biblical texts speak for themselves without any orchestral underlining, so he let the operatic text and the *mise en scène* speak for themselves and he failed in this genre, whereas in the former his principle succeeded. His square choral writing, however, was just the thing which the operas needed, but there is a complete absence of the set aria as of Ambroise Thomas upon which the singer could let himself go and the audience could marvel at his prowess.

In point of fact, we find some of Franck's best music in both *Hulda* and *Ghisèle*, particularly the former. Neither work is cyclic. There are no guiding themes or visiting cards to herald the arrival of a character or to underline a mention of his name— and this is surprising because Franck's unfailing use of cyclic material symphonically suggests that he would have been in his element with it in opera.

It is impossible to say with any accuracy that the operas are not dramatic; they *are* dramatic, but not in the sense of being sensational and the opera-goer requires sensation at all dramatic situations. It is true to say, however, that there is little to carry away. *Hulda* has been a pleasant evening at the opera. It has taken us through a story which is clearly defined and not without interest. We have listened to some excellent music, but we are not very much the wiser afterwards and neither our ears nor our eyes have been fully satisfied. Its qualities are negative where opera as a genre is concerned. Nevertheless, its visual needs are so modest, its music so easy and straightforward that, given clear diction, it would make an excellent radio opera.

It opens with a short prelude. The scene is a rocky shore in Scandinavia in the eleventh and twelfth centuries. It is night and the stage is lighted by a single torch. Hulda and her Mother are alone. There is a long scene between them. Some fishermen cross the stage, looking forward to a good night's haul as there is a gentle east wind springing up. Distant trumpets are heard and a host of Aslaks enter, proclaiming their victory over the house of Hustawick. Hulda's father has been killed. Gudleik, the Aslak Chief, sees Hulda and he orders her to follow him to his home. Hulda agrees, after swearing a terrible oath of vengeance. This brings Act One to a close.

In Act Two we are in the castle of the Aslaks. It is the wedding day of Aslak's two sons. The big hall is being prepared. Hulda enters and, in a long aria, bewails her fate. The stage is gradually filled with warriors who acclaim Hulda. It happens that Gunther, the brother of Gudleik, is to be married at the same time as Gudleik. The assembling warriors are in a state of festivity over the double wedding. Eiolf, a Scandinavian chief, joins the gathering. He is loved by Swanhilde, of the house of Aslak, but being struck by the loveliness of Hulda, he pays no attention to Swanhilde. Aslak orders a tournament, but Gudleik is troubled by the attention Eiolf is paying to Hulda. He remonstrates, but Aslak orders the tournament to begin. Hulda suddenly makes up her mind. She offers her hand to whichever of the rivals, Gudleik or Eiolf, survives mortal combat.

The crowd is horrified because the fight is now a real one and the sword points are sharp. They try to stop it, but to no avail. Gudleik falls mortally wounded. The Act closes with a long chorus of lament and woe.

In Act Three we are on a terrace. After a long and beautiful pastoral prelude, Aslak and his wife appear for a moment. The rest of the act is occupied with Hulda, who later is joined by Eiolf.

Act Four gives us the ballet without which no French opera of the period could possibly hope to succeed, after which the opera is proceeded with.

To the sounds of a purposely commonplace waltz tune played inside the castle, Swanhilde determines to win back Eiolf. She is assisted in this by Edel. Gradually she succeeds by invoking past memories, when Hulda enters and sees them. She hides and watches the passionate conquest of Eiolf. Hulda is grief-stricken and she plots revenge. Although the Aslaks have no real place for her, they hate Eiolf and agree to kill him. Eiolf and Swanhilde enter, still in the throes of love, as day breaks. They see Hulda, and Eiolf approaches her. She upbraids him for his fickleness and at her sign the Aslaks rush out and kill him. They then turn to Hulda to kill her, but she remembers her curse. They cannot understand her words and think her mad. Her vengeance completed, she throws herself into the sea.

This is a conventional enough ending for a dramatic opera and it convinces because of its straightforwardness. Hulda sings no lengthy farewell. She states her case and goes.

The chief trouble with the opera is that Hulda holds the stage too often and for too long, and the music does not rise to these situations. It does not soar and swell and is rather passionless. It is certainly more dramatic than one might have imagined it to be, but it is doubtful if Franck could have risen to any greater height even with a greater libretto. Placing it with the contemporary operas, it cannot rank with anything as theatrical as Meyerbeer, does not come up to *Carmen* and certainly falls very far below Wagner.

It takes a great composer with a strong sense of the theatre to keep our attention for any length of time while the stage is occupied by only two characters. Those who want opera to move cannot but be bored by lack of action. Although Franck's music is excellent within its limits, it does not compel attention. The singers are never allowed to let themselves go and it is unrestraint alone which can save situations that so frequently occur in *Hulda*. Franck hangs the music on to the text and leaves it to the singers to get their words over. This is not at all difficult for them, but the libretto does not lend itself to great music. It is commonplace in sentiment and banal in expression. The ability to write a great love duet is not given to all. Nevertheless, in a concert hall with minds attuned symphonically some of the duets and solo arias could well stand on their own legs.

The Marche Royale avec Choeurs and the ballet music used to be performed (sans choeurs) at the Proms. The choral writing falls between the March of the Knights in *Tannhäuser* and the Entry of the Guilds in *Die Meistersinger*. It is not as banal as the former and not as fine as the latter. This music has always been a success. Franck himself wrote to Vincent d'Indy telling him that it was much applauded; to those who would use this as a sign that Franck was actually successful during his lifetime, we would say that it was his symphonic music which lay nearest his heart and that any music even approaching the demands of ballet at that period would be bound to succeed.

This 'Ballet Allégorique' to our ears, accustomed to sophisticated ballet, to Tchaikovsky, Stravinsky, and 'Les Six', sounds very ordinary and even the graceful and not uncharming ballet of Ondines, with its pleasant chorus, dates the work. However, operatic ballet is, after all, but an interlude in the dramatic vocal moments and was never intended to be of very permanent value. This ballet music falls between two stools. It was impossible for Franck to write music which could fall gratefully on heedless ears, and yet he had to supply the need. The result is that the music is not quite good enough as music *per se*, and not banal enough for dancing purposes. Yet he himself was delighted with it and owned to his pupils that he had been dancing it himself. All this simply means that because it was outside his usual sphere, he took particular pleasure in achieving it. Other composers have been similarly deceived.

In the history of opera *Hulda* can take no place but, as has been said, there is no reason why certain of the arias (if such they can be called) should not afford welcome relief from the usual ones, hacked out so often at concerts.

When Franck died he had composed the whole of *Ghisèle* but had scored only the first act. However, he had pencilled in so many notes for the orchestration of the rest of the work that the five pupils who undertook to finish it were able to put down what the composer intended, with no uncertainty. These five pupils were Pierre de Bréville, Vincent d'Indy, Ernest Chausson, Arthur Coquard, and Samuel Rousseau. Franck commenced the composition in the autumn of 1888 and finished it in September the following year. The whole thing, therefore, came to him with the greatest ease. The libretto was by Gilbert Augustin-Thierry and the text is infinitely superior to *Hulda*. Incidentally, in the last bar but two of the original MS there is an F sharp omitted in the left hand of the piano part—but this is made up for by the omission of a B flat in the right hand part in the last bar but seven of the printed vocal score!

Ghisèle need not detain us for very long. The chief faults are those of *Hulda*. The stage is occupied for too long stretches at a time by one or two singers. It is not for some while in Act One that the composer can be recognized; the music till then might have been written by anybody. The Franck seal appears for the first time on page 52 of the vocal score and from that moment is never absent. It is most obvious in the solo or duet moments. However, all the time he seems to be anticipating the Violin Sonata and the Second Choral (so perhaps we should regard the organ work as a quotation from *Ghisèle!*). Even *Paris* is brought into use. The choruses are very ordinary shouts of triumph of warriors returned from successful wars and there is a march of dreadful banality.

In the church scenes Franck is on surer ground but even here he is not very convincing. When Ghisèle turns into a witch one thinks of Meyerbeer's perjured nuns and finds Franck's attempts at the 'Wilis' very tame. It was the old habit of letting the text and the stage action speak for themselves.

As in *Hulda*, it is in the orchestral interludes that he is most successful, moments when he could give short rein to his symphonic instincts. There is little which can be taken out of the opera and performed at concerts because it is so much better to play the purely concert music which *Ghisèle* so closely resembles. Franck tried to be dramatic on a big scale. Perhaps his failure is better than the success of Adolphe Adam and his tinkling, creaking tunes in the ballet of the same name from which there seems no escape with any ballet company. However, these two wrongs do not make a right and *Ghisèle* by Franck has no future because, unlike the ballet by Adam, it has not become a classic and never can be.

Chapter Eleven

The Songs and the Church Music

No explanation for including the songs and church music in one chapter is offered other than that both genres in the Franck canon are too insignificant in relation to his other works to warrant separate treatment. Indeed, there is hardly enough material in either to allow this. None of the most purblind admirers has ever suggested that the church music is anything but regrettable, being born of necessity rather than of inclination.

We are faced with a small number of songs which are by no means inconsequent but add nothing of importance to the literature of the genre and very little to their composer's importance, with two exceptions. These two are *La Procession* and *Paris*, the former because it is the only example of the use of a liturgical theme in the whole of Franck's output (in addition to being a very fine song outside this consideration) and the latter by reason of the circumstances of its composition. The others are by no means negligible but they lack the feeling that the texts really convinced Franck as crying out for a musical setting.

The earliest ones were composed in 1842-3. They are of an extreme simplicity. The first, *Souvenance*, dedicated to Mme Pauline Viardot, is an excellent sign of promise in a composer of but twenty-two. The line is flowing and singable and the accompaniment always carefully controlled. The song opens in F sharp minor and has a middle section in B flat minor, an early instance of Franck's latent instinct for key range. Otherwise it might have been written by Mendelssohn. However, Chateaubriand's gentle words are suitably treated. *L'Emir de Bengador* is chordal in its accompaniment and commonplace in melody and with the exception of two bars of harmonic interest at the end of the middle section, has little to commend it. *Ninon*, however, to words by Alfred de Musset, is perfectly charming. It clings rather too much to its tonic pedal point, but the delightfully airy tune is most attractive. A similar clinging to a tonic pedal point mars the middle section of Victor Hugo's *Passez, Passez toujours*, and in general the setting is uninteresting. Franck had not yet mastered the art of dealing with 6/8 time. Florian's poem *Robin Gray* introduces us to the problems of notation where we find the use of double flats which complicate a style at once simple at root. The piano part lapses into the reiterated chord technique which the period used so extensively. The best of the set, after *Souvenance*, is *Le Sylphe* (words by Alexandre Dumas) which has a cello obbligato. Here the accompaniment becomes more important in its 'ritornelli' and the cello theme is beautiful. We see an early fondness for a theme in descending thirds.

It was in 1846 that Franck wrote the simple setting to Jean Reboul's *L'Ange et l'Enfant* which his father destroyed and which served to bring him nearer to the woman who was to be his wife; the song bears the dedication 'A Madame César Franck', so that his wife received the present of this song in all its simplicity and *Les Béatitudes* in all their glory. The accompaniment is of the broken chord variety and the vocal line is too static and limited in range; however, it is difficult to see how else the words could be set and still more difficult to understand the paternal fury.

Les Trois Exiles written in 1848 appears to be a kind of patriotic song, for the cover bears the photos of Napoléon I, his son the Duc de Reichstadt, and the future Napoléon III. Vincent d'Indy gives the date as 1852, but this was the year in which the second edition was printed. M Jean Tiersot is of the opinion that the mistake was caused through the general confusion which reigned between the election of Louis Napoléon as President of the Republic and his subsequent coronation as Emperor. It is unobtainable now.

Sketches exist of a song *L'Egalité, Chant des Travailleurs* and there is also an elaborate setting for voice and orchestra of a

Hymne à la Patrie, but it is incomplete and stops short at the moment when a female chorus was designed to enter.

Les Cloches de Soir is a song of little note save that the left hand moves in the nature of the inversion of the guiding theme of *Les Béatitudes*. Otherwise the accompaniment is purely chordal.

Of the songs written for solo and for two voices over the course of years, there is a good collection in one volume which does not deserve to be ignored. Of the solo songs, *Lied* to words by Lucien Pate, has a curious augmented second and fourth in the voice part. *Le Mariage des Roses* (Eugène David) is one of the most popular, and deservedly so. It is very charming and the piano part flows easily in the first and third verses and is progressively chordal in the second and fourth.

It is in *Nocturne* (L. de Fourcaud) that we find the real Franck. It has been scored for orchestra by Guy Ropartz. Franck seems to have felt the passion of the picture very deeply and it is dramatic. The Prelude speaks for itself as pure Franck.

Ex. 164

Roses et Papillons (Victor Hugo) has an awkward right hand part. *Le Vase Brise* (Sully-Prudhomme) is less conventional and, further, has this nightmare of notation:

Ex. 165

If we consider the two-part songs at this moment it is because they are obtainable in the same volume as the preceding solos.

The pastime of domestic part-singing has long since given place to school and choir. The days when two adults went into raptures of sentiment over things like 'Oh, that we two were maying', an innocent enough sport in all truth, died with Queen Victoria and it is only now and again that we find serious duettists. Franck's songs in this form have a common failing that the piano too often doubles the voice parts in those songs which move slowly. This is not the case with *Les Danses de Lormont* where the accompaniment leaves the voices to their own devices. This is a delightful song with some imitative writing; the preceding ones have no crossing of parts and the vocal writing is square. *Soleil* gives us Guy Ropartz in the guise of a poet; here again the voices are too square, although this does not happen through the entire song. The last one in the book *La Chanson du Vannier* (A. Theuriet) is described as being for chorus or two single voices; it is more suited to the former. Here there is much more independence of lines.

There does not seem much future for any of the songs we have discussed. This, however, is not the case with two of the three which we have left till now.

La Procession is deservedly well known. Although written originally for piano and since scored for orchestra, its truest medium is the organ. The poem describes the procession of the Host across the fields, in the ceremony of blessing the crops. Charles Brisieux's poem is not more than a statement of the scene, but Franck weds it to music of great strength and reverential beauty. The voice sings over the melody of the *Lauda Sion*, the only instance, as has been said, of the use of a liturgical theme in Franck's music. The climax at the words 'Soleil! darde sur Lui tes longs rayons couchants' is one of the small inspirations which send a shiver down our backs. The arpeggio accompaniment towards the end is a little weak and the closing repetition of the opening words 'Dieu s'avance à travers les champs' unnecessary, but the song within its limits is as deeply felt as any of the greatest.

It was fitting that *Paris* should have been performed at the concert organized by the City herself during the centenary celebrations, for its purpose as a patriotic ode had passed with the lapse of years and everything about it had threatened to put it into obscurity. *Pièces de circonstances* of this nature too often disappear too thoroughly to be resuscitated.

Paris is a patriotic ode which does not rant or bang the drum. The poem by the anonymous 'B de L, Capitaine de la Garde mobile' (did he ever know of Franck's setting?) puts the words into the city's mouth as in that of an individual who has no complaint but a defence to make. As such, Franck set it to broad music with accompaniment for full orchestra. The opening phrase governs the entire song:

Ex. 166

The term 'avec noblesse' is used profusely throughout the score and is very far removed from the 'nobilmente' of Elgar. Here is no attempt to make us feel bigger and better men, and the expression is of dignity under duress.

The music proceeds with this smoothness and then changes to one of expectation.

Ex. 167

The words are not underlined in their dramatic moments but there is considerable horror in the simple straightforward setting

of the line 'la faim hideuse m'épuise'. It finishes on a note of triumph with no tub-thumping. No doubt it dates, but it is worth reviving even if only for the change it would afford from operatic arias in our concerts. It was published in 1917 but in 1947 was unobtainable except from previous stock.

Another song written about the same time was a setting of Victor Hugo's *Patria*. This also remained in MS until 1917 and is now also unobtainable. It extols nothing and the mood is subjective. It is in no way equal to *Paris* and is more the singing of one who loves his adopted country than the defiance of an invader.

Apart, therefore, from the solos written for church use, these few are the only songs written by Franck. That they are neglected is easy to understand, but there is no reason why they should be ignored. *La Procession*, at any rate, still lives and that is worth a good deal.

The church solos available separately are of completely negligible value. Settings of *O Salutaris*, *Ave Maria* and *Panis Angelicus* make us regret that the fashion of the church music of the period should have been so low. They are not as terrible as the 'sacred songs' of Gounod because they are not sentimental, but it is impossible to give them any higher praise, if what we have said can even be called praise!

I have before me some copies of Motets and Offertoires for mixed voices, including a setting of *O Salutaris* written when Franck was a boy. This is in four parts, but the greater number are in three and many have obbligato cello and harp parts. A four part setting of the Offertoire for St John the Baptist's Day has a good fugal 'Alleluia' and is an attempt to be elaborate. A similar one for the Feasts of the Virgin is depressingly banal. Why was it that as soon as composers of the period thought of Heaven, they immediately ran to harp arpeggii?

These pieces, written from necessity, can be dismissed without further comment.

I have been unable to find a copy of the *Messe Solennelle* written in 1857. However, from the Mass for three voices we can gather all the virtues and vices of Franck as a composer of utilitarian church music. Vincent d'Indy says that the work was revised constantly between 1859 and 1872, although parts of it were written when he was only choirmaster of St Clothilde. It must be remembered that this work was written in the first place for Franck's amateur choir, since money at St Clothilde was not in high enough supply for the purchase of music. What the material was like we cannot say, but the choir consisted of Soprano, Tenor, and Bass. A harp was available if required, and Franck seems to have required it on every occasion in those days. For some unknown reason it was the custom to call in a cello as well and this instrument did not simply double the organ pedals.

The Mass for Three Voices is of its period, of the days when time was no object and the Faithful were quite content to sit back and let the music put their thoughts in the right place. The Celebrant, having said the prayer to himself, took his place on the sedilia and everybody settled down in comparative comfort. The elaborate setting of the Mass, therefore, was principally an offering of the musician upon the Altar of God and through music, expressed the feelings of the congregation. There was no question of an ordinary for the Credo, for example, no traditional setting in which everyone could join. We find, therefore, in so many of the settings, considerable repetition of words and redundancy of music. The Roman Catholic Mass offers opportunities for musical drama—hence Gounod's theatricality and meretriciousness. The one thing which can be said for Franck's Mass for Three Voices is that it is not entirely theatrical and if it is commonplace, it is not tinselled. A certain charge of theatricality can, however, be levelled at the Gloria where Franck uses conventional harp arpeggii to represent the Heavenly Choir.

There are good moments in this Mass and these are invariably quiet ones. Whenever the spirit of the words called for shouts of triumph, Franck fell into a strain of vulgarity—we have seen this to be the fault with so much of the organ music. The Kyrie is quietly expressive and tends to be sentimental; it is the best movement of the whole work because of its simplicity. The Gloria is impossible for most of its course. Apart from the banality of the harp arpeggii Franck descends to the depths of theatricality at Laudamus Te when he indulges in inverted imitation of a quaver figure presumably to give some effect of bells. At Qui tollis the 'cello announces a plaintive theme which is taken up by tenor solo and chorus. There is some solid fugal writing at 'cum Sancto Spiritu' but this does not atone for the general bathos of the movement, which ends with the opening 'celestial choir'.

The Credo has a certain dignity but it lasts a very long time and is disjointed after the Crucifixus. The Sanctus, on a kind of ground, is quite impressive and the Benedictus merely states its message.

Franck interpolated his well-known *Panis Angelicus* when the work was published. This sentimental ditty has suffered many changes. Its value is set very low, but there is no reason why the BBC should allow it to be played as a trombone solo with brass band accompaniment, no matter how ardent the trombonist may be.

The Agnus Dei is of the same quality as the Kyrie, quiet and contemplative, the Dona nobis pacem being beautiful. This Mass sorely tries the loyalty of Vincent d'Indy, but it is difficult to see reason when he says that 'in spite of the musical inequality of the two works (Beethoven's *Missa Solemnis* and this one by Franck), the spirit of one must have passed into the spirit of the other with less forceful human expression, but with more divine confidence'—this apropos the Agnus Dei. It might apply to any setting.

Psalm CL is the easiest one to set. It is merely a matter of making a joyful noise. In Franck's setting everyone shouts louder than everyone else and the organ adds to the riot. As a paean of praise it has its points but its invention is practically non-existent.

One would feign have by-passed all this church music, but a study intended to be complete cannot let any genre go by, no matter how bad or indifferent, and the only thing to do is to choose the best of a bad job. It is the only instance of consistently bad music; not only is it bad church music, but it is bad as music and this charge we have been unable to level even at the operas, which we have seen to be bad operas but often good music.

Chapter Twelve

The Franck Family

It is not to be expected that all Franck's pupils should be famous or even in any way significant. Many of the names are totally unknown in this country and have, indeed, fallen into oblivion in France. There are many, however, who achieved fame in their lifetime and have maintained it, but neither the Franck family nor their descendants have ever been popular in any sense. Franck had a flair for attracting the musically intelligent, and his peculiar straightforwardness and sincerity made an instant appeal to those who followed his call. His habit was to implement his Conservatoire teaching with an evening at his own house, and although he was professor of organ, his class gradually became a kind of 'off the records' composition one. It was an understood thing that Conservatoire professors should carry on with their teaching in this manner, but as it was done gratis, many avoided doing so.

The doyen of the Franck family was Vincent d'Indy, not by any means one of the earliest disciples. His position as doyen was largely self-created. He well-nigh worshipped Franck and burned incense in a manner which allowed no contradiction. D'Indy was a curious mixture. By right he was 'Le Comte' and owned vast properties. Gradually drawn towards music, after the strictest possible unbringing, he liked to imagine himself the professional musician, willing to undertake any hack job for twenty-five francs and pretending that he was entirely dependent upon this kind of work for a living. He liked the company of instrumentalists, and M Léon Vallas, in his interesting and enlightening book, tells that he made copious lists of the names of all orchestral players with whom he was friendly. His adoption of music was met with opposition on the part of his family and although he was not disinherited, this might have happened had he not been left his grandmother's and mother's fortunes in settlement.

It was hoped that he would be an army officer. He fought bravely in the Franco-Prussian War, rising to the rank of corporal, which in those days was approximately the same as our sergeant-major. He wrote the history of his battalion during the war itself and became an authority on military strategy.

He entered the Conservatoire, going through the complete curriculum, and studying harmony and counterpoint with Albert Lavignac. He played the timpani in the orchestra at the Conservatoire and in others. Whatever his intentions may have been, he did at least go through the mill. There is something very creditable about this, and the study of his youth shows that he literally *made* himself a musician. Whether this was because of his natural inclination or the result of a too restricted upbringing cannot be guessed at, but the fact that he was willing to spend his private fortune on the furtherance of some musical ideals is all to his credit. He founded the Schola Cantorum with Charles Bordes and Alexandre Guilmant; he edited music by the old French composers; he wrote studies of Beethoven, Wagner, and Franck; he was in charge of the orchestra at the Conservatoire; he lectured; he wrote many large-scale works including operas, symphonies, symphonic poems and chamber music. All this was effected with the greatest enthusiasm. One thing he and the others learned from Franck was how to work and what that word 'work' meant. He also learned that everything had to be done to the utmost of ability and that even if others thought a work inferior, it had to satisfy the composer that it was the best he could do.

D'Indy was one of those people who started work at an hour when most other people were not considering the act of waking up. He occupied almost the whole twenty-four hours of the day, but was never averse from taking part in a festive gathering. His austere manner curiously enough fitted completely into any party, in the same way that Franck himself was able with ease to associate himself with all kinds of circumstances. His natural manner made him seem aloof and to get into the 'presence', especially if one was a foreigner, was an achievement. Once there, no one could have found a more courteous and friendly host than d'Indy.

A revolutionary against all forms of pedantry and hidebound academicism, he welcomed every kind of innovation provided that he thought it justified itself. His article on *Pelléas et Mélisande* just before that work's production was one of the most sympathetic and penetrating things ever written by anyone whose own inclinations led him in opposite directions. For d'Indy, impressionism was a thing completely foreign to his classical outlook and he flirted with it but mildly. He viewed music as something stronger than a mere approximation to an object and beneath his thought there was always a burning religiosity which was a very different thing from Franck's goodness of heart and strong faith. Romain Rolland says that one could imagine d'Indy burning heretics with fervency and zeal. Franck would have tolerated them with sympathy if not with understanding.

The catalogue of d'Indy's music is long and varied. His greatest works were the opera *Fervaal*, the Symphony in B flat, the *Istar* Variations, the Violin Sonata and the Piano Sonata. *Fervaal* has been called the 'French *Parsifal*', but it approaches that work only in its confident sincerity, and then it may be said to surpass it. Their quality is an adherence to the classical forms and an intellectual integrity which was typical of the man himself. His style does not always avoid the actual harmonic usages of Franck and it is chiefly in the matter of form that he resembles his master. Now and again there are certain twists which bear the Franck imprint but the matter is usually rather grim, which Franck's never was. He lacked the gift of spontaneous lyrical melody. M Léon Vallas tells (in *La Revue Musicale*) that d'Indy was fully aware of this and regretted it, and was overcome with pleasure because he dreamt the opening of the theme of the Violin Sonata and regarded it as a Heaven-sent sign. Cecil Gray is right when he describes him as 'a real *maître* rather than a creative artist'. The workmanship is always impeccable.

His *Cours de Composition musicale* is monumental and, further, it is interesting to read, the vista spreading far wider than the mere didacticism of the subject. In it we find the entire history of music and its development, and the whole principle is practical. However, as we have suggested, he sometimes went too far and saw in all manner of small coincidences points which he magnified to fit in with his own theories. Nevertheless, there is still no book which is so thorough in all its angles and its great feature is that it presents facts without being unduly didactic— but this was the strong point of Franck's teaching and d'Indy himself always followed in his master's footsteps at the Schola Cantorum. It was a remarkable act of faith which made him decline the chair of composition at the Conservatoire in order that he might be free to run the Schola Cantorum, the final achievement of his ambitions.

He placed the greatest emphasis on clarity, and this he obtained from his pupils by rigid attention to counterpoint. He was a great architect. He will never be a popular composer in the sense that crowds will flock to hear his works, because he falls between the stools of Gallic lightness and Teutonic seriousness, the latter sometimes approaching sententiousness. He was, nevertheless, a great man and his dual personality never hindered him in his researches and expression. If his music rarely stirs us and never makes us exult, it commands more than our respect and we can admire it.

Two stories told by M Léon Vallas may be of interest and will shed light on the difficulties of d'Indy's dual personality and his obsession with music.

The discipline of orchestras in Paris was never very strong in the earlier part of d'Indy's life, and Pasdeloup had great difficulty in keeping order at his rehearsals. D'Indy's overture *Piccolomini* was very hard for the orchestral players. In addition, its composer was a Vicomte. After the performance d'Indy was sorting out the parts when he found that a cellist had written a friendly message on one of them. 'Death to the composer! We will nip you off in the next Commune!'—and he meant it. So much for 'Art' (which d'Indy always spelt with a capital 'A') when it is not proletarian.

A great friend of d'Indy played the organ at the composer's wedding, extemporizing an Offertoire on the theme of the

Andante in Beethoven's Op. 90, at the particular request of the bridegroom. After the service, the organist asked if the Offertoire was 'all right'. 'Not bad', replied d'Indy. 'But you modulated to the sub-dominant; that is not done!'

Franck's earliest pupil and for that reason, probably, his favourite, was Henri Duparc to whom he gave piano lessons as a boy at school. Duparc returned to Franck as an adult. His life was a tragedy. In 1885 he was struck down with an incurable nervous ailment and from that moment until his death in 1933 he did not write a single note. His reputation rests upon about sixteen songs, all composed between 1868 and 1877 and they are perfect gems of French music. His symphonic poem *Lénore* and Nocturne *Aux Etoiles* are never played—the former has the literary basis of a poem by the same Bürger who wrote *Le Chasseur maudit*. Never has a reputation been formed and sustained on such a small output, and it is distressing to think of nearly fifty years spent in enforced musical silence.

Franck had three other pupils whose lives were equally tragic, Alexis de Castillon, Ernest Chausson, and Guillaume Lekeu. The Vicomte Alexis Marie de Saint Victor de Castillon (1838-73) left St Cyr to become a pupil of Victor Massé at the Conservatoire. He found Massé incapable of teaching him what he wanted, so went to Franck where he made rapid progress. He was terribly wounded in the Franco-Prussian War and died as the result of his wounds. His works are considerable. His piano concerto was hissed at its first performance owing to its novelty. It was, incidentally, played by Camille Saint-Saëns at a Pasdeloup Concert on 10th March 1872—why was Saint-Saëns unable to keep away from the detested Franck and his family? His other works include a symphony and some chamber music, none of which appears to be played anywhere now, but whose neglect is our loss. He was more than really gifted. On the foundation of the Société nationale, de Castillon acted as its first secretary.

Ernest Chausson (1855-99) started as a pupil of Massenet at the Conservatoire, but being symphonically inclined changed to the only professor capable of teaching him. Of all Franck's pupils, Chausson is the one most closely resembling him; the resemblance, in fact, is so great that we have to *look* for the signs of his individuality. These are more suggestive than positive. His music has a definitely French grace and charm, but lacks self-confidence. This is seen in the symphony which, in spite of frequent leaning forward, falls upon the similar work of Franck for its framework and construction. Further, when Franck has a choral, then Chausson must have one as well. It sounds as if Franck had for a moment returned to the happiness of *Les Éolides* and *Psyché*, indeed, the unbelievers have been known to refer to it as 'Franck No. 2'.

The workmanship is fine and the orchestral touch much more varied in its application than that of Franck, for Chausson knew and talked with d'Indy, who was a master of orchestration and of orchestral instruments. His was the most sensitive soul of all the Franckists, but this does not mean that he lacked strength. His best known works in this country are the *Poème* for violin and orchestra and the so-called Concerto for Violin, Piano, and String Quartet. The future for Chausson here is not promising because of the too close family relationship. Such were his gifts, however, that he might well have found his complete self had his life not been cut short by a bicycle accident.

Guillaume Lekeu (1870-94) was one of the few actual Belgian pupils of Franck, but he hardly had time to reap the full benefit of Franck, as it was not until 1888 that the two came together. On Franck's death, Lekeu studied with Vincent d'Indy, which was almost the same thing—'only more so', meaning that d'Indy took everything much further than Franck and left little to the imagination. Lekeu is an unknown quantity in this country, except for a Violin Sonata which is occasionally played, and which was written for Eugène Ysaÿe, and a Piano Suite. He kept his Belgian nationality to the end both in his allegiances and his music, and he may be regarded as the leading composer of that country rather than one of the many of France. His inspiration was clearly melodic and lyrical, and he laid great stress on expression. The manner was always made subservient to the matter.

Franck recognized his great gifts from the very first and it is the opinion of Ernest Closson, the Belgian critic, that had Lekeu lived, he would have outshone Franck himself. Unfortunately he died of typhoid fever before he could entirely realize himself but his works are worth playing as they mark the expansions of which the Franck idiom is capable. His *Etudes Symphoniques* rank with the high works of their period. He successfully avoided Wagner and Brahms, the prevailing influences of the time, and his works are full of the true and genuine Gallic spirit. At any rate, Belgian music is not so common that we can afford to neglect it when it keeps its own nationality and spirit. The Belgian composers of note that occur to one are Pierre Benoît, Joseph Jongen, Paul de Maleingreau, and Marcel Poot. There are others, but we do not hear them, and Lekeu is one who should be in the regular repertoire.

Whither he would have gone had not the death of Franck interrupted his studies, and his own early death cut short his career, it is difficult to judge. That he was a genius is undisputed by those who knew his music.

One of the most curious pupils must have been Augusta Holmès (1847-1903). By birth Irish, by naturalization French, she was a very tempest; Dame Ethel Smyth tells of men fleeing from her in terror—one of her works was called *Orlando Furioso!* Living in Versailles, she studied with the local organist, but he was not good enough and in 1875 she transferred herself to Paris and César Franck. The sight of these two diametrically opposed types must surely have had to be seen to be believed. However, opposing types are very often drawn to each other— Franck, Liszt, and Chabrier are a trio in point—and Augusta undoubtedly got inspiration from the quietness of Franck in the way that Franck was stimulated by the tempestuous Augusta. She was a composer of some note and made her mark in Paris concerts. She evidently composed 'con fuoco'. In 1878, in the competition organized by the City of Paris, she was placed next to the winners, Dubois and Godard, while in 1880 her choral work on the Iliad, *Les Argonautes*, received honourable mention. In 1885 she was herself one of the judges in the competition. She composed a 'Triumphal Ode' for the Paris Exhibition of 1889 and a *Hymn to Peace* for the Dante Festival held in Florence in 1890. She invaded the Paris Opéra in 1895 with *La Montague Noire*, but she had had to wait fifteen years for production. She wrote three other operas.

Sir Henry Wood produced *Irlande* in London, describing it as 'finely scored'. This work gave away her nationality by its rhythms, although not based on Irish themes.

That she made inroads on the hearts of the other Franck pupils may be imagined, but d'Indy records that she was too overwhelming for him! Dame Ethel Smyth in an entertaining essay in *A Final Burning of Boats* quotes Camille Saint-Saëns as saying 'we were all in love with her'—at last he must have found something congenial in the Franck ménage! Dame Ethel quotes her *Hymne à Aphrodite* as being something outstanding and Gustav Mahler said that it was as immortal as *Tristan*. In spite of her French milieu she remained the wild Irish rebel and her personality swayed all who came into contact with her. She must have enlivened the weekly gatherings at Boul' Mich 95.

Other composition pupils were Charles Bordes (1863-1909) who, with Guilmant and Vincent d'Indy, founded the Schola Cantorum with the primary purpose of reviving the study of choral music, but which in time became a general institution for musical training. He made a specialized study of Basque Folk music, wearing himself out in propagating the gospel of music all over France; Arther Coquard (1846-1910) who, after writing a large number of full-scale works, became a critic; Camille Benoît (1851-1923) who gave up music for the post of Curator at the Louvre; and Gaston Vallin, possessed of such self-criticism that he destroyed everything he wrote as none of it reached the ideal at which he aimed.

As a matter of national interest, Franck also included amongst his pupils John Hinton (1869-1932) the authority on organ construction.

We put it on record that although H. C. Colles in Vol. 7 of the *Oxford History of Music* describes Paul Dukas as a Franck pupil, this is not so. Dukas never studied with him.

Franck's organ pupils held appointments in the leading Paris churches. Of these Gabriel Pierné (1863-1937) succeeded him at St Clothilde. Later he succeeded Colonne as conductor of the orchestra of that name. He wrote a vast amount of music—nine operas, nine ballets, choral works and at least four orchestral suites. Henri Dallier (1849-1934) was organist at Rheims Cathedral before going to Paris to study with Franck and Bazin. He held the appointments at St Eustache and the Madeleine, succeeding Gabriel Fauré in 1905 when Fauré became Director of the Conservatoire.

The most noted was Louis Vierne (1870-1937) whose organ symphonies and pieces are the natural development of Franck's harmonic background. He acted as assistant to Widor at St Sulpice and later held the appointment at Notre-Dame, where he died in harness.

The two surviving pupils of Franck, Pierre de Bréville and Guy Ropartz, merit special consideration and it is interesting to realize that they had this direct contact. The former (born in 1861) studied with Dubois at the Conservatoire before going to Franck. His life has been varied both as composer and critic, in the latter capacity on the staff of *Mercure de France*. His compositions include a Lyric Drama *Eros Vainqueur* and a suite *Stamboul*. The fact that they have not provoked any issues does not imply that they are negative. His critical writings are noted for their penetration. As professor at the Schola Cantorum he wielded a good influence. His music may lack the force of Vincent d'Indy, but it has just the qualities which d'Indy lacks and is full of charm and intensity of a subdued nature.

Guy Ropartz (born in 1864) has lived his life mainly outside Paris. He became Director of the Conservatoire at Nancy in 1894 and in 1919 moved to Strasbourg where he directed the Conservatoire and the Concerts. He entirely reorganized the system of teaching at the Conservatoire there and brought it into line with that of Franck and the Schola Cantorum. This has been one of the most striking influences of the Schola. He has composed mostly in the big forms, but has also written much poetry, and a lyric drama. His works include four symphonies and three operas. He has been drawn largely to Breton folk tunes and has incorporated them in his music. The latest work, his fifth string quartet (composed in 1947), is a model of conciseness and design. It is delightfully fresh.

These two men in their eighties are as alert as the average mind of forty. Their handwriting is as firm as that of a man approaching middle-age. They are in the direct line of the Franck tradition and hold an honourable place in French music. That we do not hear their music in this country is our loss, but there seems to be a fear of the Franck tradition, largely

1829

Schola Cantorum

founded upon a theory that it is all too derived and bears the stamp of its ancestry too clearly. This is not the case and both these composers have marked originality.

It is fitting here to consider in some detail the practical living example of the influence of César Franck, an example which as far as can be ascertained, is unique. There have been many great teachers who have also been composers of eminence but whose influence has been directed almost solely on those with whom they came in personal contact. Their 'system', so to speak, has been centralized in this way and although their successors may have attempted to initiate a kind of apostolic succession, it has been limited in scope. The Schola Cantorum, now the Ecole César Franck, is this practical living example, but at its inception it had other ideals.

It was founded for the purpose of reviving the study and practice of church music, and in this respect succeeded in revitalizing an art which had sunk into the decay of unenlightened routine. It will be remembered that Franck himself was curiously ignorant of and uninterested in the liturgical music of the church and the music of the sixteenth century. Guilmant and Bordes had vision. They saw a field capable of expansion and whatever may have been the faults of Guilmant as a composer, he must be allowed to have been gifted with a sincerity and enterprise which was most commendable and outstanding. Bordes was one of those ardent propagandists who were tireless in the fulfilment of their ideals. Vincent d'Indy was a musician of importance who had the energy and enthusiasm to give the enterprise sufficient personal, knowledgeable, and, be it added, financial backing.

A large building was found in the Rue Stanislas, in Montparnasse, which opened its doors in 1896. This house had been the headquarters of the English Benedictines who came over to France with James II, and it had been a prison during the Reign of Terror. It was almost a matter of honour among the personnel to answer any inquiry as to what the building was by giving it its revolutionary description, especially when the sounds of mixed music could be heard; it is on record that an English inquirer was much impressed with the French prison system...

The studies were solfège, Gregorian chant, vocal ensemble, organ, 'clavier', harmony and counterpoint and there were six professors. Eventually the premises proved too small and a move was made to the present building in the Rue St Jacques. Vincent d'Indy became the official director, and in his inauguration address on 2nd November 1900 he propounded the policy which was to be followed. The principles were to be that of César Franck and the chief study was ancient music, especially Gregorian chant. D'Indy expressly stated that since Franck's pupils liked to consider themselves as members of one family, so, it was hoped, would the students of the Schola Cantorum, which was 'a little piece' of Franck. Amongst the high ideals to which the aim was directed was the lifting up of general musical knowledge. D'Indy quoted Adolphe Adam as telling his pupils that he got no joy out of music and wrote it only because he could do nothing else. He also told the story of a Prix de Rome winner who, on hearing the opening bars of the Allegretto of Beethoven's Seventh Symphony, exclaimed aloud: 'Ah, that's pretty! It is worthy of Saint-Saëns.' The lesson was that in a big institution there could not be very much personal contact or interest taken in the students, whereas in a small one everyone could know everyone else.

One of the most important works undertaken by d'Indy in the name of the Schola was the editing, publishing, and performing of works by the ancient French and Italian composers, and what is now called 'musicology' played a leading part in the curriculum. Such works as Rameau's *Guirlande* and Monteverdi's *Orfeo* were produced with considerable success and aroused great interest.

The Schola became an institution for the teaching of all musical subjects, not in competition with the Conservatoire—indeed, d'Indy took over the orchestra there, saying that there was no reason to make music 'against anyone'—but with the view to the furtherance of symphonic music on the basis of César Franck. Amongst the original professors were Blanche Selva, Albeniz and Grovlez for piano, Jane Bathori for singing, Pierre de Bréville and Albert Roussel for counterpoint, Maurice Emmanuel for musical history, and Alberic Magnard for extra composition. The early students included Roussel, Déodat de Séverac, Erik Satie and Roland-Manuel. The Schola got the reputation of being revolutionary and several pens inveighed against it. With his detestation of anything to do with Franck

Camille Saint-Saëns was in the forefront of these. In *Les Idées de M Vincent d'Indy*, Saint-Saëns railed against the theories of d'Indy as expressed in his monumental *Cours de Composition musicale* and against his two *bêtes-noirs*, Wagner and Franck, Saint-Saëns's dictum being 'For myself, Art is, above all, Form', a needless and not very convincing principle, since the two are indivisible.

However, the Schola thrived on its rivals and opponents, slowly spreading its influence to other areas of France, to such places as Nancy, Strasbourg, Rouen, Brest, and Bordeaux, and crossing the borders of Switzerland. The Schola attracted many foreign students.

Another strong feature was the performance of works by professors and students of the institution itself, not at the expense of outside composers but in the light of showing the world what was being accomplished within its walls. Thus the Schola was flourishing when Vincent d'Indy died in 1931. In his will d'Indy left the Schola Cantorum to Louis de Serres (a pupil of Franck), and Guy de Lioncourt (a pupil of d'Indy), the appointment of Director and Deputy Director being left to the Advisory Committee to decide. The committee elected the former as Director and the latter his deputy. A certain faction, however, thought otherwise, and after a stormy meeting it set aside the election as directed by the will and decided by the committee. There was a complete rupture. The majority of the staff of the Schola followed de Serres and de Lioncourt, founding the present Ecole César Franck. For some time the school lived a nomad life, eventually finding its present quarters at 3 Rue Jules Chaplain, where it has finally settled. M Guy de Lioncourt is now the Director.

Thus the continuity is maintained. As Franck did not enforce his will or theories on his pupils, so it was ever the principle of d'Indy and his successors to enforce nothing direct upon the students. Nevertheless, the mould is clearly marked upon the compositions of the students.

The École César Franck, therefore, is a lasting example of the influence of a great man, an influence strong enough to carry weight with those born after Franck's death. Individual teachers influence individual students, but are there any other permanent institutions which propagate a gospel to this extent?

Chapter Thirteen

Franck's Contemporaries

WHEN he died in 1890, Franck had out-
lived all those composers alive when he
himself was born, and who were to become representative, with
the exception of Verdi, Gounod, and Ambroise Thomas. These
died in 1901, 1893 and 1896 respectively. The position of music
in France in 1890 was infinitely better than in 1822. Apart from
the Franck pupils who have been discussed in the previous
chapter, French music had become established. It is true that
the most prominent names were not all of the highest quality,
but with a few notable exceptions, French music at their hands
had become something intensely personal.

The majority of Franck's colleagues at the Conservatoire
were not noteworthy as composers, with the exception of Leo
Delibes, Ambroise Thomas and Jules Massenet. The first may be
said to have formulated something supremely French with his
ballets, of which *Coppélia* and *Sylvia* will remain in the theatre
until the last ballet dancer has worn out the last shoe. If it is
true that the traditional choreography has worn a trifle thin and
the music remains simply to charm, there is no denying its
exquisite polish and fitness. The trouble is that the movements
we like to hear are so short; but this must always be the case
with music which is written for a purpose and in collaboration
with another art. The second is known in this country solely as
the composer of *Mignon*, and a perverted version of *A Midsummer Night's Dream* adapted for operatic purposes. In this respect
his operas were never more than coloratura vehicles in which
the text was of little importance, and the music of little value
provided that the singers had the usual opportunities. Thomas,

therefore, marks the descent from Rossini and closes an epoch. In his eighty-five years he accomplished much and was a person of some note.

In the way that Spontini and his decorations denoted a recognition of musicians as a glory to their country, so Ambroise Thomas wore the Grand Cross of the Legion of Honour, granted in 1851 on the occasion of the thousandth performance of *Mignon* at the Opéra-Comique, and he was the first musician to be so honoured: in the same year Verdi brought him in person 'le Grand Cordon des Saints Maurice et Lazare' on behalf of the King of Italy. Thus music had become a strong social force. In England Queen Victoria had knighted Henry Rowley Bishop —but that was another thing.

Thomas's activities were not confined to the theatre and he wrote a number of large *oeuvres de circonstances* which are not heard of today. A venerable old man, he simply could not move with the times, but in spite of Vincent d'Indy's account of his lack of appreciation of Franck, and Thomas's own admission of bewilderment, he did not work against what is called progress; being unable to keep up with it, he let it pass him, but never did he interfere with or try to suppress the advanced ideas of his professor of organ.

Of the three, undoubtedly the most important was Jules Massenet, and it will be noted again that these three composers were primarily concerned with the theatre. Massenet's operas supplied a foil to the pretentiousness of Wagner which was threatening to swamp French opera; although in many ways his music shows the influence, it lacks anything which can be said to savour of strength. He was prolific and never pretended to write anything but what he knew the public wanted. His sincerity has been doubted. M Léon Vallas tells us that for many years he was one of Vincent d'Indy's idols. However, d'Indy asked how he had been able to find music which 'appeared heavenly' in his oratorio *Marie-Madeleine*. Massenet replied that he did not believe in any of it, but 'the public likes that kind of thing, and we should always be at their bidding'. D'Indy was so shocked that such a subject could be treated cynically that he never forgave Massenet.

It is customary to sneer at the rather sickly sentiment of

199

Massenet's subjects and tunes, but he possessed a sense of the theatre and considerable dramatic force. If the writer may recount a personal experience—many years ago he was 'twiddling the knob' of his wireless set and suddenly came upon an opera from Paris which thrilled him. He could not place it but the whole thing sounded intensely dramatic and moving. To his surprise, the announcer said that it was a performance of *Thaïs*. This is not to say that the writer immediately read all the operas of Massenet, but he acquired a new respect for their composer. Massenet was one of the few of Franck's colleagues to like him personally and appreciate his music, and this Franck realized. Perhaps it would be too unkind to describe Massenet as 'a purveyor of opera to the public taste'. As a teacher at the Conservatoire he was superb.

Other colleagues were Victor Massé, whose sole achievements were light operas, Ernest Guiraud and Albert Lavignac. Guiraud was a composer of light operas but at the same time was a learned and authoritative professor. His greatest achievement was the scoring of *Les Contes d'Hoffmann*. He died suddenly in the Secretary's office at the Conservatoire. Albert Lavignac had the Wagner virus in his very vitals. His book shows the librarian's mind in its wealth of detail. He numbered Vincent d'Indy amongst his pupils, a fact which the pupil had a tendency to forget. He had a reputation of being an easy-going professor. One other deserves mention, Théodore Dubois, who, it will be remembered, had the vision to recommend Franck for the chair of organ at the Conservatoire. A prolific composer, his works are now dead, if, indeed, they were ever alive, but they included operas and large-scale choral works. He became Director of the Conservatoire and resigned as a consequence of the 'affaire Ravel'.

The leading figure in French music, whose resources enabled him to travel all round the world, thus becoming a kind of self-appointed characteristic French composer, was Camille Saint-Saëns. Enough has been said in these pages as to his personal propensities. His musical attributes were a facility and slickness which far outshone his powers of inspiration. Now and again he had flashes—*Samson et Dalila* is still a good opera—and his piano concertos are exceedingly well written, pleasant to listen to (if one does not want to think) and grateful to play. His organ works are fresh and original and in their pseudo-classical manner occupy a place of comparative importance. There was one besetting sin. Saint-Saëns was a snob. In his memoirs he unblushingly genuflects at the action of Queen Alexandra in pouring him out a cup of tea 'with her imperial and royal hands'. Having acquired a habit of poking his nose into everything and everywhere, he asked if he might write a Coronation March for the 1901 Coronation; being the representative French composer in this country—they knew no better in those days of Brahmsian influence—he was accepted at a Three Choirs Festival with an oratorio *The Promised Land* which must be heard or read to be believed for its dullness.

The trouble with Saint-Saëns was summed up cleverly by Debussy. 'M Saint-Saëns knows more about music than anyone else in the world. His profound knowledge, however, has prevented him from ever subjecting it to his own personal desires.' And 'Does no one care sufficiently for Saint-Saëns to tell him that he has written music enough and that he would be better employed in following the belated vocation of explorer?' This last thrust was at Saint-Saëns's tendency to write pseudo-music about every country he visited.

Saint-Saëns in his early days showed signs of being the Saviour of French music, but he fell under the Teutonic influence which weighed him down too much. His abilities were too slight to make him Wagnerianly pompous, but he tried to superimpose a Teutonic seriousness on to a Gallic lightness, and succeeded in becoming quickly out-dated. As an ambassador it would have been better had he acted as the agent of his betters.

He is the opposite number to Vincent d'Indy in some respects. The latter had the seriousness and the erudition. The former had all the knack and tried to be self-consciously pretentious. D'Indy was never pretentious, although he had all the possibilities.

Three other names amongst the older composers, two of them the friends of Franck's own generation—Edouard Lalo, Emmanuel Chabrier and Georges Bizet—were outstanding. We have already referred to the importance of Lalo's Symphony in G minor, coming, as it did, just at the time of Franck's and of Saint-Saëns's 'avec orgue'. His *Symphonie espagnole* for violin and orchestra avoids the technical needs of a concerto without sacrificing its display. He is remembered here chiefly by this work and his two *Aubades* which are of the company of Delibes, as is the ballet *Namouna*. His opera *Le Roi d'Ys* is one of those works which hold the stage by their charm rather than by their drama, while the two-act Ballet *Namouna* is a classic. At the beginning of his career he specialized in chamber music.

Emmanuel Chabrier, doughty champion of Franck, earthy, ebullient, and bluff, has the unfortunate fate of being known for a work which he did not write. The *España* Rhapsody is based on Spanish national airs. He dished them up for piano, and someone else scored the result. His piano pieces are distinctly original because although they are piano music of their own peculiar type, they seem to have been thought out orchestrally. Indeed, the *Pièces Pittoresques* which form the nucleus of the ballet *Cotillon*, are more satisfactory in this form. The style of the piano is chordal and never lyrical—he himself was a heavy player. His opera *Gwendolen*, with the noisiest overture on record, is fine music; but Chabrier became a whole-hearted Wagnerian and could not conceal it—it is curious to imagine the early Wagner enthusiasts as being considered 'ultra-modern'.

Georges Bizet's *Carmen* is one of the most important operas ever written. Perhaps it is a little too slight to have been used as a foil to Wagner which Nietzsche and others considered it.

The oratorios of Franck have their seamy parallels with those of Charles Gounod. *La Rédemption* and *Mors et Vita* were considered by their composer as being his greatest achievements, his offering upon the Altar of the Christian Church. It is difficult to choose between the two and the sickly, sentimental sacred songs like *Oh, Divine Redeemer*. Gounod took himself very, very seriously. For an entertaining story we again go to M Léon Vallas.

Gounod was brought to the Avenue de Villars to meet Vincent d'Indy. Immediately on entering the room he went to the piano and played three Ds very solemnly and slowly. He looked at d'Indy, who made no comment. Gounod played the Ds again and d'Indy began to feel uncomfortable. Once more the keys were struck, even louder and heavier than before. 'Young man', said Gounod, 'do you know what that is?' D'Indy recognized it only as three Ds, but felt that there must be something else to it; before he could say anything, Gounod solemnly remarked 'It is the motive of Eternity'. As d'Indy had never thought of Eternity in that manner he felt a little awkward and surprised until he realized that the notes formed the opening of Gounod's cantata *Gallia!*

The fault with all Gounod's sacred music lies in its maudlin sentimentality and vulgar secularity. It is true that now and again *La Rédemption* has a certain breadth but it lacks individuality and style. Franck detested Gounod's music and it is not difficult to understand the reason. It lacks the ring of sincerity. Franck's *Rédemption* may have its weaknesses, but these are more in construction than in feeling. It is as the composer of *Faust* that Gounod will live. *La Reine de Saba, La Nonne sanglantée* and all his other fertile writings are dead and buried.

These were the foremost of Franck's working contemporaries, and it is interesting to realize that during his life there occurred the birth of the complete re-orientation of French music in the person of Erik Satie, a revolution of which Franck was probably quite unaware although the unconscious precursor of it, for the early Satie has many of the Franck characteristics of harmony The three streams of French music flow from Franck, Massenet, and Satie. From the first comes the embryo line of symphonists, commencing with Albert Roussel, a student of the Schola Cantorum; from the second the 'school' of Gabriel Fauré and his illustrious pupils; and from the third everything which has appeared in French music during the last twenty-seven years. A concert of Satie's music in the BBC's Third Programme explained his neglect. Were he ever to become widely popular and played, he would put out of court 'Les Six' and all those composers who have come to be recognized as representative of this century. This is not to say that this French music is inferior, it merely shows that the Satie idiom and style are not capable of expansion, any more than are the highly systematized formulas of Schönberg and Webern capable of variety, and the same applies to all formularized thought from Albrechtsberger to Ebenezer Prout, and onwards. These last have all led to dead-ends and the Central Europeans are rapidly approaching theirs.

The value of the Franck outlook lies in the fact that it was never dogmatic and always elastic, and the same may be said of Fauré, although in many ways it was rather limited.

Impressionism has its origins in Franck—see *Les Éolides*—tentative though they may have been. They were never evolved from Satie or from Massenet. While Roussel tightened the Franck mould, Fauré refined the Massenet sentimentality and 'Les Six' repeated the later Satie.

The composers considered representative of French music in the earlier half of the present century—Gounod, and Saint-Saëns—have by now been relegated to their proper perspective of derivation. After them came the emphasis on Debussy and Ravel, two widely differing æsthetics, to be succeeded by 'Les Six'. The canvas is now being broadened.

Chapter Fourteen

The Man—Summary

An aura of sanctity and mysticism sur-
rounds the person of César Franck. It is
traditional that he was so completely and intensely spiritual, so
wrapt up in the Mystery that his life was one long and unre-
lieved posture of genuflection. According to the general belief,
he could hardly have been human.

There is absolutely no authority for this legend. It arose because in contrast to the prevailing fashions of his day, he was
full of sincerity and honesty, and completely self-effacing. The
evidence against all this mystical humbug is to be found in his
music and in his daily habits. M Guy Ropartz who as a pupil
knew Franck well, says that he was 'essentially a good man,
preoccupied with searching in his own work and in that of every
other composer for all that was beautiful; this was his æsthetic
doctrine. He was perfectly sociable. He was deeply religious but
in no way bigoted. He was serious (but not solemn) and absolutely disinterested. I never heard him say anything unkind
about anyone and never a bitter word on the subject of the
neglect of his works.' M Pierre de Bréville confirms this, empha-
sizing his honesty. How, therefore, has this legend become
established?

When M Guy Ropartz described the theme of the Allegretto
of the Symphony as 'the motif of faith', he did so because the
quality of the theme is firm, bright, and happy, knowing that
Franck himself was the happiest and friendliest of men. He did
not so describe it because it was a slowly moving dirge. Debussy
referred to him as 'this intensely good man' and did not in any
way suggest a mystical or spiritual background.

The sign of the devout believer is a supreme happiness and contentment, and an unbounded optimism. One has only to mix with those who have adopted the religious life without its ascetic qualities to realize that among them one finds all these things in their most complete form, no matter to what sect they belong. Franck was an ardent Roman Catholic. The sacrifice of the Mass was something very real to him. He was present at it not only as officiating organist but as a worshipper. He dedicated his genius to the Real Presence which he knew to be there. In this belief nothing could shake him. Everything he wrote, every organ extemporization (and during the course of each service he played many) was a tribute to the greater glory of God.

It does not take a man filled with mysticism and spirituality to refrain from evil speaking, lying, and slandering. Many such live far removed from a religious atmosphere, and the man next door may as well be canonized as any priest. Franck practised what he believed out of church as well as in it. The Christian tenet 'Love thy neighbour' was a command that he obeyed by instinct. He loved the Lord his God because he knew that his gifts sprung from Him.

He would have gone to church had he not been an organist and would have believed implicitly in everything. His music would still have had its ring of deep sincerity. Had he really been more than human, so absolutely spiritual as to be not of this earth, a saint in fact, sent down from Heaven expressly for saintship, he could never have written anything approaching cheapness or vulgarity, and this inability is not borne out in his music, witness, for example, the second subject of the Finale in the *Prélude, Aria, et Final* or the *Final* in B flat.

Franck was always gregarious and Vincent d'Indy is quick to point this out; but tradition would have us believe that he never went out in the evening and held converse with no one, the type of man who 'doesn't drink, doesn't smoke, and goes to church'. All this has resulted from taking Gallic enthusiasm too literally. M Alfred Cortot doubts the mysticism ascribed to Franck:

'Not that I subscribe for my part to the favourite legend of a mystic César Franck, a sort of Pater Seraphicus lost in dreams of Heaven, illumined with the ecstatic contemplative fervour

which removed him from the pricks and realities of life. The
nobility of Franck's life, reflected perfectly in the beauty of his
work, was precisely that he neither shook off reality nor despised
the affairs of humanity, but rose above them. And however ur-
gent and overwhelming they might sometimes be, he never
allowed them to dim the sacred flame of inspiration, nor weaken
within him his passionate love of music.'

M Cortot also draws attention to Paul Valéry's essays on
Pascal and Leonardo da Vinci in which he 'deprecates the
motive that allows us to confuse the actual man who creates a
work of art with the man suggested by that work of art'. This
has happened in the case of Franck and a moment's thought will
remind us of other cases, Roussel for example, whose musical
creative violence was so very different from his mildness of
personality.

The testimony of M Guy Ropartz is unquestionable and
must carry the full weight of authority. That Franck was a man
of deep human sincerity has never been denied; that he was a
man of deep religious feeling and belief has been distorted into
something altogether too superhuman. His pupils called him
'Pater Seraphicus' because of his benign countenance and manner, not because he necessarily opened his lessons with prayer.
He has become an object of prejudice in the eyes of a country
fundamentally not Roman Catholic, naturally self-conscious,
and reticent in its enthusiasms unless of the mob variety. Not
for Franck the theological library owned by Bach. His faith was
a matter of course and taken for granted. His music, charged
with a religious impulse as deep and sincere as that of Bach, has
been tarred with the same brush as its composer. To write everything to the greater glory of God, like Bruckner, like Elgar (when
it was not the British Empire), like Franck is something which
the Englishman keeps to himself. There was no cant about
Franck. He was an exceptionally kind man, with sufficient
breadth of vision to allow him to look for every beautiful moment in every work, no matter whether written by friend or foe;
he liked to welcome his friends at any hour and would extend
similar hospitality to any of his evil-wishers had any called on
him. He loved music with an intense and burning passion. It is
significant that Debussy, who did not hesitate to rend hip and

thigh composers who were antipathetic to his æsthetic ideals,
saw what was behind *Les Béatitudes* and in spite of the fact that
the musical expression and import of the work were very different from his own, wrote praisingly of it.

Upon whom, therefore, lies the blame for this legend? Upon
the most faithful disciple, Vincent d'Indy, who, as M Léon
Vallas says, created a myth about himself as a professional
musician and a similar one about Franck as a spirituality. It is
d'Indy, whose book so far has been the only one accessible in
English, who has given us this view and, knowing no better,
we have taken what he said as gospel. Rarely has 'Heaven
defend us from our friends' been such a truism. With the best
will in the world, Vincent d'Indy must take the blame for this
charge. Once we have put his adoration, and to a smaller extent
that of his friends into their right perspective and have found
the level, then Franck appears as he truly was and his music
speaks for itself as music, and not as a kind of theological
document.

Let us have done, therefore, once and for all with this humbug
and cease to be prejudiced against this very ordinary man (not
particularly cultured outside music, but inside it, a genius of the
first water), with musical as well as human frailties and appetites.

The life of Franck offers a parallel with that of Bach. Both
men lived a humdrum existence; both were confined to organ
lofts for their living and both were compelled to teach all their
lives; both had indifferent material upon which to work; their
choirs were amateur and they had to write for whatever resources lay to hand. If we find that Bach was lucky in this respect
(judging from his cantatas) it does not belittle Franck in any
way that his material was indifferent. Both wrote their organ
music for their respective instruments. It is no disparagement
to say that both were domesticated in so far as they loved their
families and their homes. So far as spirituality goes, it is hard to
see why this should be a matter for opprobrium with the composer of *Les Béatitudes* and not for that of the *B minor Mass* or
the *Passions*, and, indeed, not for the composer of the *Mass in D*
—for spirituality has never been laid at the door of Beethoven.

The parallel with Elgar is more real because Elgar was of our
time. He was also deeply religious and only a convinced

Christian could have composed *The Dream of Gerontius*; whether this stricture can be confined to Roman Catholics is something which cannot be proved because no other composer can ever set the poem. Yet the charge of spirituality at the expense of worldliness has never been laid at Elgar's door. The 'Elgar Stakes' is one proof of his worldliness, and Elgar playing bridge at the Savile Club is paralleled by Franck at the Opéra bouffe. Their religiosity, to use an ugly word, did not stand in the way of their respective enjoyments, although of the two Franck appears to have been the more gregarious.

Franck might have written *The Apostles* (we have seen several points of contact in the chapter on the choral works) but he could not have written *The Dream of Gerontius*, simply *because it is too spiritual*. *Les Béatitudes* deals with a philosophy and not with metaphysics. There is more spirituality in the work of Elgar and in the Fifth Symphony of Vaughan Williams than in any work by Franck, for spirituality implies an adoration which does not seek to preach a gospel. In *Les Béatitudes* Franck preached a gospel which he wished the world would adopt. The other two concentrated on the direct worship of something mystical.

The fact that both Franck and Elgar failed hopelessly when attempting to delineate anything evil is of no significance.

Elgar was of a generation of musicians who were thinkers. One could not regard Sir Hubert Parry when Director of the Royal College of Music in the same light as Ambroise Thomas when Director of the Paris Conservatoire. Franck was surrounded with flippancies and artificiality. Elgar had as his contemporaries men who were establishing the musician as a social force and were making music if not one of the learned professions at least one of the seven liberal arts and sciences. The probity of Elgar, therefore, had not Franck's background against which it could shine.

To read the lives of Franck and Elgar is to read of two forms of disillusion. According to his biographers Elgar's life was one of complete frustration and dismay. Franck was frustrated only outside himself and he was never dismayed.

Although he never showed the least resentment at his neglect as a composer, Maurice Emmanuel suggests that this was a kind of cloak behind which he concealed his feelings. After the first

o

performance of the symphony, when the hall was in almost complete silence he said to his friend Paul Poujaud 'What magnificent sonority! And what a reception!'. Now, was this a state of mind into which he had doped himself, was it pure naïveté, or was it that he really did imagine the applause? Was there not something really rather noble which fought fiercely with his natural feelings? Composers have often said that there seemed to be no applause when in point of fact it had been terrific, their state of mind being non-receptive at the time. Possibly it may work the other way, and to one not accustomed to vociferation the applause of the few may sound magnified.

That he was sensitive to his own achievements is shown in the story told by Henri Cochin in Chapter Four. Maurice Emmanuel has another one. On one occasion he was delighted with a new work by one of his pupils. After the performance the pupil walked home with Franck. On saying good-bye, Franck repeated his congratulations and on putting the key into the door, the pupil heard Franck murmur, 'I, too, have written some beautiful things'. Was this another form of defence? In any case the attitude shown by Franck all through his life was truly admirable, whether real or feigned.

The spirit of resignation which the philosophy of the Sermon on the Mount inculcated was of a more durable quality than that of Aristotle and Kant to which Reicha endeavoured to live and which failed him at his most critical moment. This we can see in the frenzy of the hysterical letters which he wrote when a change of government threatened the production of his opera *Nathalie* at the Paris Opéra.

In 1943 the writer felt constrained to send a diffident letter to one of our leading composers whose new work had moved him considerably. The composer replied 'I am not one of those who do not like praise'. Franck was like that. He hated anything which savoured of sycophancy or insincerity, but when any of his pupils or friends expressed a genuine opinion, if it was favourable, his large face beamed all over; if unfavourable, he promptly went into the matter like any student and tried to find out the reasons.

If ever there was an instance of the infallibility of the philosophy of Psalm 118 Verse 22, Franck provides the example. It is customary to think of all pioneers as faced with obstacles and lack of appreciation. If we examine the situations of the great composers, we shall find that only a very few suffered the neglect which faced Franck. Bach and Schubert are the only ones to which this can apply. Handel's bankruptcies were due more to lavish ventures than to dislike on the part of the public. The others may have lived in comparative penury, but they had little difficulty in making the money. Wagner was extravagant but he always had his successes. Franck had no real triumph until his sixty-eighth year. True it was that some of the audience burst into applause after the Prelude of the *Prélude, Fugue, et Variation* when it was performed in its arrangement for piano and harmonium, but he immediately squashed it by saying that the movements were joined together and please, no applause yet!

The position with Debussy is one of the most curious in the history of music. Between the Impressionists and the Franckists there is a great gulf fixed, with nothing in common to bridge it except a love for music. Debussy's adventures with Franck ended in disaster and he let loose his poisoned darts in every direction which displeased him, especially towards those who, he felt, were hypnotized by the word 'symphony', and by those he meant the Franckists. He disowned his early *Fantaisie* for Piano and Orchestra because it had the savour of the Franckian classical approach and the cyclic form. Yet he never spoke of Franck or d'Indy without the deepest respect. He referred to the former as amongst the great musicians. 'It is well, amidst pressing preoccupations, to think of the great musicians, and, above all, to bring them to the thoughts of others. I have chosen to pay homage to one of the greatest on Good Friday, for I feel that this homage is in keeping with the idea of sacrifice evoked by the greatness of the man and the sanctity of the day.'

Although he was not whole-hearted in his praise for *Les Béatitudes*, finding the choruses 'too facile in their dramatic quality', he regretted that one should have to hear Franck's very individual melody set to verses that would disgrace a mouth-organ. He emphasized Franck's sincerity and compared him favourably with Wagner in this respect—it so happened that *Les Béatitudes* had been preceded by some of the *Rheingold* music at a Concert Lamoureux. 'The discovery of one beautiful harmony sufficed to make him happy for a whole day'—so wrote Debussy who seemed to find in the music of Franck the repose that his soul lacked. It is certain that Franck could have given Debussy the necessary philosophy had the two not been so far apart æsthetically. In one respect Debussy made a mistake. 'The action of César Franck on French composers does not really amount to much; he taught them certain processes, but their inspiration has no connection with his.'

What Debussy meant was that French composers have not all received their impulse from the same source as Franck received his. The actual musical influence, however, has been immense, and in all fairness to Debussy we must remember that the time had scarcely been long enough for it to make itself felt. However, it can hardly be said that a composer whose teaching principles have been perpetuated in an institution like the Schola Cantorum and at the Conservatoires in Nancy and Strasbourg does not amount to much. Debussy himself was aware of his own originality and individuality, but the latter was the stronger of the two. Debussy derived direct from Franck, Satie, and Ravel. Of the later evidence of the Franck influence outside his immediate pupils there is the example of Albert Roussel, a pupil of Vincent d'Indy at the Schola Cantorum with sufficient individuality to use his own technique, which is a clear extension and development of the teaching at Boul' Mich 95. Franck's 'processes' lay chiefly in the matter of form and we have M Pierre de Bréville's testimony that this was by example and not by precept. Some composers have 'systems' and 'processes', thumb-nail directions for the manufacture of music by the ungifted and unendowed. Who ever heard of Beethoven's 'system'? The followers of these mechanics always present a depressing sight, from those of Ebenezer Prout onwards. With their hats in their hands they produce pastiche after pastiche with not even the inkling of any imagination or creative urge. The present day inheritors of the Franck tradition show their ancestry through their own individuality, and even the symphony of Chausson, slavish imitation of a model though it is, shows its genuine feelings. In any case, every copyist must reach a dead-end—sooner rather than later.

Franck's influence is seen in Elgar and, to a limited degree in Delius. With the latter we see it in the splashes of wood-wind colour and the holding up of the movement, as in *In a Summer Garden*. It is not of great significance and may well be accidental.

Elgar's sliding chromaticisms and sequences are derived direct from Franck. Melodically Elgar appears at first sight to have more line, but examination shows that the 'Nimrod' variation, for example, bears a close relationship to Franck in his habit of slightly varying a fragment. The 'infinite melody' of Franck can be found in a work like *The Music Makers* where the music goes round and round in the way of *Psyché*. *The Apostles* bears the Franck chromaticism and in a passage like 'Sanctus, Fortis' in *The Dream of Gerontius* Elgar leans heavily on Franck's shoulders. Other points of contact need not detain us but, in passing, the deeply felt Roman Catholicism of the two composers may imply an affinity; this is an open question and depends on the point of view of the reader.

Although both composers were highly stylized, Elgar was the more mannered and the less varied. Whether hymning the British Empire or trying to soar above the earth, he did both in more or less the same way. Franck never sounds tired; Elgar often gives the impression of being terribly laboured. The emotional appeal of both is great and is not dissimilar, except that Elgar makes a call on nobility with which Franck was not concerned. Elgar makes us think we are fine fellows; Franck has rather the opposite effect. Elgar did very much the same thing for music in this country that Franck did for it in France. Unfortunately Elgar used a foreign way of thinking and did not formulate a national idiom. Elgar's influence on British composers has been infinitely less than that of Franck on French ones and it is not till we come to the symphonies of Vaughan Williams that we find a definite English language.

There are few composers so completely varied that they can hold our attention unswervingly, but we return to Franck again and again, finding renewed hope and inspiration.

When we think of the industry of this great man, the routine never varied, and the neglect and rebuffs which he suffered at every turn, we have an example which all should follow. Those who say that teaching spoils their natural facility and freedom

213

and protest that they can compose only when the conditions and circumstances are at their best (which usually means a private income) should ponder this life which we have studied. Franck liked teaching, but there are always pupils who are not bright and the lessons are a continuous concentration and restraint. Franck had many of these, but he kept his ideals in their view. Whatever he did, he did to the utmost of his ability, and the most elementary pupil received the scrupulous attention which he gave to Vincent d'Indy, Guy Ropartz, Pierre de Bréville, Ernest Chausson and others.

What was it which buoyed him up in all his humdrum existence? The knowledge that the hour would come when he could relax at his MSS and deal with the work in progress. What buoyed him up in the face of his disappointments? His firm, healthy faith, a faith which some might call dope because it engendered confidence in himself. This faith made him succeed where others have failed. It gave him contentment of mind and kept his eye on the ultimate goal. It drove away any thoughts of jealousy which might well have been expected to attack him and it caused him to view the successes of his contemporaries with the greatest pleasure. Perhaps it taught him to 'turn the other cheek'. Who else would have persisted in his loyalty to Saint-Saëns who never had a good word to say for him? Yet there are the dedications to his 'friend Camille Saint-Saëns.' If Saint-Saëns had a conscience it must have hurt him at every turn.

The really good men are rarely noticed in their lives, but the good is not always interred with their bones. No evil lived after Franck; there was none. It was that his contemporaries were incapable of understanding or realizing him and when enlightenment came, it was too late.

What Berlioz did for the orchestra and Wagner for the theatre, so did Franck for symphonic music. All three composers may be called the founders of modern music.

Books Consulted

César Franck	Vincent d'Indy
Debussy	Edward Lockspeiser
The Theories of Claude Debussy	Leon Vallas
Franch Piano Music	Alfred Cortot
A Final Burning of Boats	Ethel Smyth
A Survey of Contemporary Music	Cecil Gray
Oxford History of Music, Vol. VII	H. C. Colles
The Choir	
Musical Times	
Dictionary of Music and Musicians	Grove
Dictionary of Modern Music and Musicians	A. E. Hull
Everyman's Dictionary of Music	Eric Blom
The Oxford Companion to Music	Percy Scholes
Liszt	James Huneker
César Franck. Personal Reminiscenes	J. W. Hinton
Cours de Composition musicale	Vincent d'Indy
César Franck	Maurice Emmanuel
Antonin Reicha	Maurice Emmanuel
Vincent d'Indy—La Jeunesse	Leon Vallas
Déodat de Séverac	Blanche Selva
Le Sonate	Blanche Selva
La Schola Cantorum	Vincent d'Indy and others
Camille Saint-Saëns	J. Bonnerot
César Franck ('Les Musiciens célèbres')	Auguste Serieyx
La Revue musicale	
Monsieur Croche	Claude Debussy
Musique française de Franck à Debussy	Paul Landormy
La Musique et Les Musiciens	Albert Lavignac

List of Works

The compilation of this list has been a difficult task to arrange chronologically. The catalogue in Vincent d'Indy's book is incomplete and inaccurate. Recently (1947) a number of MSS have been presented to the Bibliothèque nationale by the composer's grand-daughter, but there are many gaps in the opus numbers.

The works mentioned in Part One of this Appendix are all in MS with one exception, and are quoted for the first time out of France.

Part Two is an amended version of Vincent d'Indy's list.

PART ONE

WORKS WRITTEN BEFORE 1841

Op. 5	1834	Variations Brillantes sur l'air du 'Pre aux Clercs' for piano
Op. 6	1834	Grand Trio pour piano, violon, et violoncello
Op. 8	1834 to 1835	Variations brillantes sur le Ronde favorite de Gustave III for piano Accompaniment for 2 flutes, 2 oboes, 2 clarinets, 2 bassoons, 2 horns, and strings
Op. ?	1835	*O Salutaris.* Published 1922 by La Revue Musicale for mixed chorus and organ
Op. 10	1835	Première Grande Sonate for piano
Op. 11		Deuxième Grand Concerto in G minor for piano Orchestra 2 flutes, 2 oboes, 2 clarinets, 2 bassoons, 2 trumpets, 4 horns, 3 trombones, timpani, and strings
Op. 12	18	Première Grande Fantaisie for piano
Op. 13	18	Première Symphonie a Grand Orchestre
Op. 14	18	Deuxième Fantaisie for piano
Op. 15	18	Deux Melodies for piano
Op. 18	18	Deuxième Sonate for piano
Op. 19	18	Troisième Grande Fantaisie for piano

The year of composition cannot be stated in every case.

The following MSS of works written later are included in Part One because they have no date. They are to be found either in the Bibliothèque nationale or the library of the Paris Conservatoire.

'Hymne à la Patrie'
for voice and orchestra
'Justus it palma florebit'
for bass, chorus, and organ
'Gratias super gratiam'
for chorus
'Tunc oblati sunt'
for chorus
'Sinite parvulos'
for solo voice
'Laudate pueri'
for chorus
'Plainte des Israelites'
for chorus and orchestra
'Cantique de Moïse': Cantemus Domino
for chorus and orchestra
Symphonic Interlude from *Rédemption*
(the original version)
Grand Choeur
for organ
'Marlborough'
for chorus and 'mirlitons'
Polka
for piano
Deux Melodies—à Felicité
for piano
Stradella—Opera, MS
for voices and piano only.

PART TWO

WORKS WRITTEN AFTER 1841

(Those marked * are apparently unobtainable)

Op.	1	1841	Trois trios concertans	Schuberth
			No. 1 in F sharp	
			No. 2 in B flat (Trio de Salon)	
			No. 3 in B	
Op.	2	1842	Quatrième trio concertans	
Op.	3	1842	Eclogue	Schlesinger*
			for piano	
Op.	4	1842	Duo on 'God save the King'	Schlesinger*
			for piano, four hands	
Op.	5	1843	Grand Caprice	Lemoine
			for piano	

Op. 6	1843	Andante quietoso for piano and violin	Lemoine
Op. 7	1843	Souvenir d'Aix la Chapelle for piano	Schuberth*
Op. 8	1844	Quatre melodies de Schubert transcribed for piano	Chaillot
Op. 9	1844	Ballade for piano	Unpublished
Op. 10	1844	Solo de piano, with string quartet on a theme from 'Ruth', com- menced in 1843	Unpublished
Op. 11	1844	Première fantaisie sur Gulistan for piano	Costallat
Op. 12	1844	Deuxième fantaisie sur l'air et le Virelat 'Le Point du Jour' de Gulistan	Costallat
Op. 13	1844	Fantaisie for piano	Presumed never written
Op. 14	1844	Duo pour piano et violin concer- tans sur Gulistan	Costallat
Op. 15	1845	Fantaisie pour piano sur deux airs polonais	Costallat
Op. 16	1845	Trois petits riens for piano	Unpublished
Op. ?	1845 to 1846	'Ce qu'on entend sur la montagne' symphonic poem, after Victor Hugo, for orchestra	Unpublished
Op. 17	1846	Duo à quatre mains sur 'Lucille' de Gretry for piano, four hands	Pacini-Bonaldi*

No opus numbers.

1843 to 1846	*Ruth* Biblical eclogue for soli, chorus, and orchestra	Heugel
1842 to 1843	Songs Souvenance Ninon L'Emir de Bengador Le Sylphe (with cello obbligato) Robin Gray	Costallat
1846	Song 'L'Ange et l'Enfants'	Hamelle (published in 1878)
1851 to 1852	*Le Valet de Ferme* Opera in three acts	Unpublished
1853	Song 'Les trois exiles' for baritone and bass	Mayaud*
1858	Messe solennelle for bass solo and organ *O Salutaris* (published separately)	Regnier-Canoux*

	1858	Andantino for organ	Costallat
	1858	Accompagnement d'orgue	Leclerc
	1858	*O Salutaris* for soprano and tenor	Noel
	1858	Trois Motets No. 1 *O Salutaris* for soprano and chorus No. 2 *Ave Maria* for soprano and bass No. 3 *Tantum Ergo* for bass	Noel
	1859	Trois Antiennes for organ	Heugel
	1859	Hymn *Le Garde d'honneur*	Noel

Some opus numbers restored but there is some confusion over Op. 12, 16 and 17.

Op. 12	1860	Messe à trois voix for soprano, tenor, and bass, with organ, harp, cello and double bass accompaniment	Bornemann (taken over in 1872)
	1860 to 1862	Six Pièces pour grand orgue	Durand (taken over in 1879)
Op. 16		Fantasie (in C)	
Op. 17		Grande pièce symphonique	
Op. 18		Prélude, fugue et variation	
Op. 19		Pastorale	
Op. 20		Prière	
Op. 21		Final	
Op. 22		Quasi marcia for harmonium	Leduc

No further opus numbers

	1863	Cinq pièces pour harmonium	Leduc
	1863	*Ave Maria* for soprano, tenor, and bass	Bornemann
	1865	*La tour de Babel* Oratorio for soli, chorus, and orchestra	Unpublished
	1865	*Les plaintes d'une poupée* for piano	Mangeot
1869 to	1879	*Les Béatitudes* Oratorio for soli, chorus, and orchestra	Joubert
	1870	Patriotic Ode *Paris* for voice and orchestra	Roudanez (published in 1917)*
	1871	*Patria* for voice and orchestra	Roudanez (published in 1917)*

219

1871	Trois Offertoires	Bornemann
	No. 1 *Quae est ista*	
	for soli, chorus, organ, and double bass	
	No. 2 *Domine Deus in simplicitate*	
	for 3 voices, organ, and double bass	
	No. 3 *Dextera Domini*	
	for soli, three-part chorus, organ, and double bass	
1871	Song *Le Mariage des roses*	Enoch
1871	*Domine non secundum*	Bornemann
	for soprano, tenor, and bass	
	Quasi fremuerunt gentes	Bornemann
	for three-part chorus, organ, and double bass	
1871	Offertoire on a Breton air	Nauss
	for harmonium	
1871	*Redemption*	Heugel
	Poem-symphony for soprano, chorus, and orchestra	
1872	*Panis Angelicus*	Bornemann
	for tenor, organ, harp, cello, and double bass	
1872	Song *Passez, passez toujours*	Costallat
1872	Song *Roses et papillons*	Enoch
1872	*Veni creator*	Hamelle
	for tenor and bass	
1873	Song *Lied*	Enoch
1873	Prélude, fugue et variation	Durand
	Transcription for harmonium and piano	
1874	*Rédemption*	Heugel
	Second edition, with new Symphonic Interlude and male chorus	
1876	*Les Eolides*	Enoch
	Symphonic poem for orchestra	
1878	Trois pièces pour grand orgue	Durand
	1. Fantaisie (in A)	
	2. Cantabile	
	3. Pièce héroique	
1878 to 1879	Quintet in F minor	Hamelle
	for piano, 2 violins, viola, and cello	
1879	Song *Le vase brisé*	Enoch
1881	*Rebecca*	Heugel
	Biblical scene for soli, chorus, and orchestra	
1882	*Le Chasseur maudit*	Lemoine
	Symphonic poem for orchestra	
1884	Song *Nocturne*	Enoch
1884	*Les Djinns*	Enoch
	Symphonic poem for piano and orchestra	

1884	Prélude, Choral, et Fugue for piano	Enoch
1882–1885	*Hulda* Opera in four acts	Choudens
1885	Variations symphoniques for piano and orchestra	Enoch
1885	*Dance Lente* for piano	Schola Cantorum
1886	Sonata for violin and piano	Hamelle
1886 to 1887	Prélude, Aria, et Final for piano	Hamelle
1887–1888	*Psyché* Symphonic poem for chorus and orchestra	Bornemann
1888	Hymne for four male voices	Hamelle
1888	Cantique	Unpublished
1888	Song *La Procession*	Leduc
1888	Song *Les Cloches du soir*	Leduc
1888	Psalm CL for chorus, orchestra, and organ	Breitkopf and Hartel (posthumous work)
1888	Six Duos for equal voices 1. L'ange gardien 2. Aux petits enfants 3. La vierge a la crèche 4. Les danses de Lormont 5. Soleil 6. La chanson du vannier	Enoch
1886–1888	Symphony in D minor	Hamelle
1888	*Le premier sourire de mai* for three female voices	Hamelle
1889	Andantino for grand organ	Costallat
1889	Préludes et prières de Ch. V. Alkan Arranged for organ in three books	Costallat
1889	Quartet in D minor for two violins, viola, and cello	Hamelle
1888–1890	*Ghisele* Opera in four acts	Choudens
1889–1890	L'Organiste for harmonium	Enoch
1890	Trois Chorals for organ No. 1 in E No. 2 in B minor No. 3 in A minor	Durand
	44 petites pièces for organ or harmonium	Enoch (published as 'Pièces Posthumes' in 1900)

Index

(Compiled by J. Nicholas Demuth)

A

Adam, Adolphe, 17, 21, 46, 162, 177, 196
— Louis, 21
Ad nos (Liszt), 28
Air écossais, 15
Albeniz, Isaac, 196
Albrechtsberger, 203
Alceste (Gluck), 20
Alexander (Handel), 46
Alexandra, Queen, 201
Alkan, Charles, 52
Audantino, 112
Ange et l'Enfant, L', 24, 179
Apostles (Elgar), 168, 171, 209, 213
Après-Midi d'un Faune, L' (Debussy), 64
Argonautes, Les (Holmès), 192
Aristotle, 16, 210
Athalie (Mendelssohn), 157
Athenaeum, 40
Aubades (Lalo), 202
Auber, Daniel, 12, 13, 21, 46
Augustin-Thierry, Gilbert, 177
Aux Etoiles (Duparc), 190
Ave Maria, 183

B

Bach, Johann Sebastian, 17, 28, 37, 46, 48, 52, 59, 84, 87, 95, 99, 102, 111, 112, 120, 121, 145, 149, 156, 169, 207, 208, 211
Ballade irlandaise, 15
Balzac, Honoré de, 16
Barbier de Séville, Le (Rossini), 12, 13
Bathori, Jane, 196
Batiste, Antoine, 95
Béatitudes, Les, 25, 31, 32, 35, 36, 39, 41, 42, 43, 52, 92, 110, 120, 156, 159, 160, 163–171, 179, 180, 208, 209, 211
Beatrice et Benedict (Berlioz), 52
Beethoven, Ludwig van, 13, 15, 20, 35, 37, 40, 45, 46, 52, 54, 55, 56, 57, 59, 72, 84, 88, 97, 124, 132, 139, 141, 143, 145, 171, 187, 190, 196, 208, 212

Bellaifue, Camille, 38
Benvenuto Cellini (Berlioz), 46
Benoist, François, 20, 21, 33, 34, 163
Benoît, Camille, 193
— Pierre, 192
Berlioz, Hector, 11, 12, 16, 17, 19, 21, 46, 52, 66, 69, 80, 159, 161, 214
Berton, Henri, 21
Bibliothèque Nationale, Paris, 7, 61, 120, 172
Bishop, Sir Henry Rowley, 13, 199
Bizet, Georges, 34, 201, 202
Blau, Edouard, 160, 162
Bloody Nun, The (Gounod), 39
Boëllmann, Léon, 79
Boëlly, Alexandre, 95, 156
Boïeldieu, François, 12
Bonn, Electoral Orchestra, 15
Bordes, Charles, 187, 193, 195
Boris Godunov (Mussorgsky), 36
Bornemann et Cie, 9
Boult, Sir Adrian, 87
Boutarel, 38
Brabançonne, La, 42
Brahms, Johannes, 40, 47, 51, 58, 72, 83, 84, 86, 88, 98, 124, 126, 127, 128, 130, 132, 141, 145, 163, 167, 192
Brand, Paul, 40
Brave New World (Huxley), 92
Bréville, Pierre de, 7, 34, 54, 55, 85, 89, 176, 194, 196, 205, 212, 214
Brisieux, Charles, 181
British Broadcasting Corporation, 80, 185
——— Third Programme, 203
Bruckner, Anton, 207
Bürger, Gottfried, 66
Busoni, Ferruccio, 149
Bussine, Romain, 32
Byrd, William, 29, 30

C

Cantabile (*Trois Pièces*), 35, 48, 110–111, 112, 121
Cantique de Moïse, 159
Carillon (Elgar), 32

Carmen (Bizet), 175, 202
de Castillon, Alexis, 32, 71, 190
Cavaille-Coll, Aristide, 27, 105
Ce qu'on entend sur la montagne, 25, 55, 59, 61–64, 129
Chabrier, Emmanuel, 23, 28, 39, 40, 192, 201, 202
Chanson du Vannier, 181
Chant, Anglican, 29
Chasseur maudit, Le, 37, 38, 41, 50, 67–69, 93, 190
Chateaubriand, François-René, Vicomte de, 179
Chausson, Ernest, 41, 57, 176, 190–191, 212, 214
Cherubini, Luigi, 12, 15, 16, 18, 19, 20, 21, 45, 46
Cheval de bronze, Le (Auber), 12
Chevillard, Camille, 42
Choir, The, 29
Chopin, Frédéric, 12, 21
Chorals, Trois, 40, 43, 50, 59, 72, 85, 104, 112–118, 120, 177
Christ lag in Tödesbanden (Bach), 111
Christmas Oratorio (Bach), 161
Clark, Scotson, 29
— London Organ School, 29
Clémont, Félix, 41
Cloches de Soir, Les, 180
Closson, Ernest, 191
Clothilde, St., 27, 28, 33, 35, 41, 42, 43, 52, 87, 96, 104, 120, 121, 122, 184, 193
Cochin, Henri, 52, 210
Colles, H. C., 163, 193
Colomb, Mme, 164
Colonne, Edouard, 35, 41, 193
— Society, 42, 193
Comoedia, 122
Concertans, Trois Trios, 21, 123–129
Concerto for Violin, Piano and String Quartet (Chausson), 191
Concertstück (Weber), 13
Conservatoire, Paris, 7, 12, 14, 15, 16, 17, 18, 19, 22, 23, 24, 33, 34, 35, 36, 37, 40, 41, 42, 45, 46, 47, 96, 105, 171, 186, 187, 189, 190, 194, 196, 198, 200, 209
— Liége, 14, 42
Conte Vénitien (Demuth), 98
Contes d'Hoffmann, Les (Offenbach), 37, 200
Coppélia (Delibes), 198
Coquard, Arthur, 176, 193
Cortez, Fernand (Spontini), 12
Cortot, Alfred, 13, 38, 43, 152, 206, 207
Cotillon (Chabrier), 202

Couperin, François, 96
Cours de Composition Musicale (d'Indy), 56, 101, 188, 197
Covent Garden, London, 13
Creation (Haydn), 46
Critique of Pure Reason (Kant), 27
Crotch, Dr William, 12

D

Dallier, Henri, 40, 42, 193
Dame Blanche, La (Boïeldieu), 12
Danse Macabre (Saint-Saëns), 69
Danses de Lormont, 181
Daussoigne-Méhul, Louis Joseph, 14
David, Eugéne, 180
— Felicien, 24
Debussy, Claude Achille, 11, 47, 62, 64, 66, 165, 201, 204, 205, 207, 211, 212
Defoe, Daniel, 29
Delibes, Leo, 34, 40, 41, 197, 202
Delius, Frederick, 213
Derepas, Gustave, 93
Désert, Le (David), 24
Desmousseaux, Mme Josephine, 21, 24
— Wife of Composer, 26
Dickens, Charles, 29
Dies irae (Saint-Saëns), 79
Dimitri (Jonçières), 36
Djinns, Les, 37, 69–71, 145
Dobson, Monica, married Georges, son of composer, 29
— Robert, 30
Dohnányi, Ernst von, 79
Don Giovanni (Mozart), 20, 46, 64
Donizetti, Gaetano, 21, 46
Dream of Gerontius (Elgar), 166, 209, 213
Dubois, Théodore, 33, 39, 40, 47, 192, 200
Dukas, Paul, 193, 194
Dumas, Alexandre, 179
Duo based on God Save the King, 23, 144
Duparc, Henri, 31, 89, 163, 170, 190
Dupuis, Sylvan, 42

E

Eclogue, 23, 144
Ecole César Franck, 197
— royale de Musique, L', 14
Egalité, Chant des Travailleurs, L', 179
Eisteddfod, 29
Elévation (*Pièces Posthumes*), 119
Elgar, Sir Edward, 12, 32, 166, 168, 171, 182, 207, 208, 211
Elijah (Mendelssohn), 168

Elizabeth, Queen of the Belgians, 42
Emir de Bengador, L', 179
Emmanuel, Maurice, 25, 33, 121, 122, 172, 196, 209, 210
Employés, Les (Balzac), 16
L'Enfance de Christ (Berlioz), 161
Eolides, Les, 35, 43, 50, 51, 64–66, 85, 89, 90, 91, 140, 163, 191, 204
Erl King (Schubert), 127
Erostrate (Reyer), 98
Eros Vainqueur (de Bréville), 194
España (Arr. Chabrier), 202
Etudes Symphoniques (Lekeu), 192
Eulenberg, 86
Euryanthe (Weber), 13
Expert, Henri, 30, 51

F

Fantaisie (Debussy), 47, 211
— *Première Grande,* 15, 144
— *Six Pieces,* 28, 97–101, 102, 121
— *Trois Pièces,* 107–109, 112, 115
Fauré, Gabriel, 194, 203, 204
Faust (Berlioz), 52
— (Gounod), 39, 203
Fervaal (d'Indy), 188
Fétis, François, 15, 16
Fielding, 29
Figaro (Mozart), 20
Final Burning of Boats (Smyth), 193
Final (Six Pièces), 47, 106–107
Florian, 179
Flotow, Friederich von, 172
de Fourcaud, L', 180
Fra Diavolo (Auber), 12
Franck, César Auguste
1822–1837 :
     Birth, 13. Student at Liége Conservatoire, 14. First compositions, 14–15. Concert tour, 15. Student under Reicha, 15–17. Commencement of friendship with Liszt, 17.
1838–1871 :
     Student at Conservatoire, Paris, 18–22. *Trois Concertans* published by subscription, 21. Family moves to Brussels, 22. Commencement of *Ruth,* Family moves to Paris, Franck becomes organist at Notre-Dame-de-Lorette, 23. *Ruth* performed at Conservatoire, Composition of *Ce qu'on entend sur la montagne,* 25. Marriage, 26. Composition of *Le Valet de Ferme.* Becomes organist at St.-Jean-St.-Francois-au-Marais and choirmaster at St. Clothilde; composi-
tion of *Six Pièces,* 28. Unsubstantiated report of visit to England, 29. Composition of *La Tour de Babel,* and *Paris;* Franco-Prussian War, 31. Foundation of Société de Nationale de Musique; second performance of *Ruth,* 32.
1872–1890 :
     Organ appointment at the Conservatoire, 33. Composition and performance of *Redemption;* composition of *Les Eolides* and *Trois Pièces,* 35. Performance of *Quintet; Les Béatitudes* completed and performed, 36. Awarded Légion d'Honneur; *Rébecca, Le Chasseur Maudit, Les Djinns* and *Prélude Choral et Fugue* completed and *Hulda* commenced, 37. *Hulda* completed; *Variations Symphoniques, Violin Sonata* composed; *Prélude Aria et Final, Psyché* completed and performed; *Symphony* commenced; ' Franck Festival ', 38. Unfinished Opera, *Ghisèle,* commenced; first performance of *Symphony,* 39. *String Quartet* composed and performed. Accident and Death, 40.
1922 :
     Centenary Celebrations, 41–43
Franck, Edouard 15
— Georges, 29
— Germain, 30
— Jérome, composers' brother, 13
— Joseph, 13, 22
— Festival, 38
Freischütz, Der (Weber), 13, 46
French Piano Music (Cortot), 38, 152
Fugues, Trente-six, pour le pianoforte, Composées d'après un nouveau système (Reicha), 16

G

Galleotti, Cesare, 42
Gallia (Gounod), 203
Garçin, Jules, 39
Gaspard de la Nuit (Ravel), 155
Gaubert, Philippe, 42
Georges Chapel, Windsor, St., 122
Ghisèle, 39, 173, 176–177
Gigout, Eugène, 42, 96
Glinka, Michael, 12
Gloria (Pièces Posthumes), 119
Gluck, Christoph von, 20
Godard, Benjamin, 192
Gossec, François, 12
Goss, William, 29

Gounod, Charles, 12, 16, 52, 156, 163, 183, 184, 198, 203, 204
Grace, Harvey, 82, 168
Grand Choeur, 120
— *Concerto en Si mineur*, 61
Grande Pièce symphonique (*Six Pièces*), 101–102, 121
— *Sonate, Première, Pour le Piano Forte*, 15, 143
— — *Deuxième, pour piano*, 15, 54, 55, 144
Graner Messe (Liszt), 38
Gray, Cecil, 171, 188
de Greef, Arthur, 41
Grétry, André, 12
Grove's Dictionary of Music and Musicians, 25, 40, 54, 82, 168
Grovlez, Gabriel, 196
Guillaume Tell (Rossini), 21, 46
Guilmant, Alexandre, 95, 96, 112, 118, 120, 121, 187, 193, 195
Guirard, Ernest, 37, 39, 40, 41, 200
Guirlande (Rameau), 196
Gwendolen (Chabrier), 202

H

Habeneck, François, 45, 46
Halévy, Jacques, 16, 21, 46
Hamelle et Cie, 86
Handel, George Frideric, 17, 30, 45, 46, 52, 156, 211
Haydn, Joseph, 11, 46
Heldenleben, Ein (Strauss), 58, 64, 94
Hinton, John, 30, 157, 193
Holmès, Augusta, 192–193
Honegger, Arthur, 125
Hopkins, Dr E. J., 29, 30
Hugenots, Les (Meyerbeer), 12, 13
Hugo, Victor, 25, 32, 37, 61, 69, 179, 180, 183
Hulda, 37, 38, 39, 173–176, 177
Hummel, Ferdinand, 14, 19
Huneker, James, 25
Huxley, Aldous, 92
Hymne à Aphrodite (Holmès), 193
— *à la Patrie*, 180
Hymn to Peace (Holmès), 192

I

Idées de M. Vincent d'Indy, Les (Saint-Saëns), 197
Imitation of Christ The (A Kempis), 93
In a Summer Garden (Delius), 213
d'Indy, Vincent, 13, 25, 32, 36, 38, 40, 42, 50, 53, 54, 55, 56, 57, 58, 59, 71, 74, 76, 79, 92, 93, 98, 101, 122, 124, 126, 130, 139, 141, 144, 157, 159, 163, 166, 169, 172, 176, 179, 183, 186–190, 191, 193, 194, 195, 196, 197, 199, 200, 201, 202, 203, 205, 208, 211, 212, 214
— Comtesse Rezia, grandmother of Vincent, 21
Irlande (Holmès), 192
Israel in Egypt (Handel), 162
Istar Variations (d'Indy), 188

J

de Jangevitch, Tatiana, 42
Jonçières, Vincent, 36
Jongen, Joseph, 192
Joseph (Méhul), 32, 52, 156
Judas Maccabeus (Handel), 46
Juive, La (Halévy), 46

K

Kant, 16, 27, 210
Keats, John, 90

L

Lalo, Edouard, 36, 41, 79, 80, 98, 201
Last Judgement (Spohr), 162
Lauda Sion, 181
Lavignac, Albert, 187, 200
de L., B., Capitaine de la Garde Mobile 31, 182
Leborne, Simon Aimé Ambrose, 18, 54, 124
Lefébure-Wély, Louis James, 95, 111, 112
Légion d'Honneur, 37, 199
Lekeu, Guillaume, 190, 191–192
Lemmens, Nicholas, 95
Lénoire (Duparc), 190
Leseur, Jean, 17
Library, Queen Victoria's, London, 8
— Royal, 30
Lied, 180
Liége, 12, 15, 41
— Conservatoire, 14, 42
de Lioncourt, Guy, 197
de Lisle, Leconte, 64
Liszt, Franz, 12, 16, 17, 18, 22, 23, 25, 28, 38, 47, 52, 54, 55, 58, 63, 66, 69, 70, 72, 80, 124, 128, 145, 149, 162, 192
Louis XVIII, 15, 33
Lulli, Jean Baptiste, 46

M

Magic Flute (Mozart), 46
Magnard, Alberic, 196
Magnificat, 40

Mahout, 42
de Maleingreau, Paul, 192
Manon (Massenet), 158
Marche aux Flambeaux (Clark), 29
Mariage des Roses, Le, 180
Marie Madeleine (Massenet), 35, 160, 199
Marmontel, Antoine, 16, 18
Marseillaise, La, 42
Marty, Eugène, 42
Masaniello (Auber), 12
Massé, Victor, 37, 190, 200
Massenet, Jules, 33, 35, 39, 40, 52, 158, 160, 190, 198, 199, 200, 203, 204
Mass in D (Beethoven), 13, 46, 171, 208
—— —— *for Three Voices*, 183–185
Mathew Passion, St (Bach), 46, 208
Méhul, Etienne, 14, 32, 46, 52, 156
Meistersinger (Wagner), 176
Mélodie, 15
Mendelssohn, Felix, 12, 45, 46, 72, 157, 168, 178
Menestrel (Boutarel), 38
Mennier, Jules, 42
Mephisto (Liszt), 69
Mercure de France, 194
Messe Solennelle, 183
Messiah (Handel), 46
Meyerbeer, Giacomo, 12, 13, 21, 25, 29, 46, 69, 166, 168, 175, 177
Meyer-Lutz, Wilhelm, 29
Michel 95, St., Boulevard, 26, 28, 31, 43, 193, 212
Midsummer Nights' Dream (Thomas) 198
Mignon (Thomas), 48, 198, 199
Minister of Fine Arts, 36, 37
Monde Artiste (Torchet), 38
Montague Noire, La (Holmès), 192
Monteverdi, Claudio, 196
Montrouge, 40
Mors et Vita (Gounod), 202
Motets et Offertories, 183
Mozart, Wolfgang Amadeus, 46, 72, 73, 84, 125
Music Makers (Elgar), 213
Musical Times, 29, 64, 122
Musiciens de la Renaissance, 42
de Musset, Alfred, 179

N

Namouna (Lato), 202
Natalie (Reicha), 16, 210
Niedermeyer, Abraham, 46, 120, 172
Nietzsche, Frederich, 202
Nimrod (Elgar), 213
Ninon, 179
Nocturne et Procession, 42, 180
Nonne Sanglantée, La (Gounod), 203

O

O Salutaris, 183
Offenbach, Jacques, 12, 26, 37
Offertoire pour la Messe de Minuit (*Pièces Posthumes*), 119 ; F minor, 119 ; G minor, 119
Office, Public Records, 30
Olympie (Spontini), 12
Onslow, George, 21
Opéra, Paris, 16, 18, 41, 45, 46, 172, 192, 199, 210
— Bouffe, 26
Orchestra, Liverpool Philharmonic, 87
— B.B.C. Symphony, 87
Orfeo (Monteverdi), 196
Organiste, L', 119
Orgelbüchlein (Bach), 111
Orlando Furioso (Holmès), 192
Orientales, Les (Hugo), 69
Our Lady Star of the Sea, Church of, 30
Overture for orchestra in ⅝ time (Reicha) 16
Oxford History of Music, 163, 193

P

Palestrina, Giovanni, 51
Panis Angelicus, 183, 185
Paris, 8, 31, 32, 42, 51, 163, 177, 178, 181–183
Parratt, Sir Walter, 122
Parry, Sir Hubert, 209
Parsifal (Wagner), 34
Pasdeloup, Jules, 38, 39, 189
Passez, Passez toujours, 179
Passions (Bach), 208
Pastorale (*Six Pièces*), 28, 50, 103–104, 107, 108, 117, 121
Pate, Lucien, 180
Pathétique Sonata (Beethoven), 56
Patria, 32, 183
Paul et Virginie, 94
Pelléas et Mélisande (Debussy), 188
Pergolesi, Giovanni, 46
Philharmonic Society of London, 13
Piano Concerto in A minor (Hummel), 19
— *Concerto* (Brahms) D minor, B flat, 72, 98, 136
— *Sonata* (d'Indy), 188
—— — (Brahms), 58
— *Sonatas* (Beethoven), 56
— *Suite* (Lekeu), 191
Piccolomini (d'Indy), 189
Pièce Héroïque (*Trois Pièces*), 43, 108, 111–112, 121
Pièces Pittoresques (Chabrier), 202
— *Posthumes*, 118, 119
— *d'Orgue, Six*, 28, 97–107, 112

Pieces, Trois pour Grand Orgue, 35, 107–112, 163
Pierné, Gabriel, 41, 42, 87, 122, 193
Plainte des Israélites, 159
Pleyel, Ignoz, 21, 36
Poème (Chausson), 41, 191
— *de l'Extase* (Scriabin), 80
Polkas, two, 26
Poot, Marcel, 192
Potter, Cipriani, 13
Poujaud, Paul, 210
Prélude, Aria et Final, 38, 59, 125, 150–155, 205
— *Choral et Fugue*, 37, 59, 131, 145–149, 150, 159
— (*Six Pièces*) *Fugue et Variation*, 28, 102–103, 121, 145, 159, 211
Préludes, Les (Liszt), 55, 63, 64, 80
Prière (*Six Pièces*), 105–106
Printemps (Debussy), 165
Procession, La, 51, 178, 181, 183
Promised Land (Saint-Saëns), 201
Prout, Ebenezer, 203, 212
Psyché, 42, 65, 88–94, 126, 191, 213
Purcell, Henry, 29

Q

Quartet, 94, 125, 138–142
— (Schumann), 138
Quintet in F minor, 35, 36, 42, 52, 64, 130–133, 134, 163
Quintet (Schumann), 136

R

Rabaud, Henri, 42
Rameau, Jean Philippe, 46, 196
Ravel, Maurice, 11, 12, 58, 66, 72, 155, 200, 204, 212
Rebecca, 37, 171
Rédemption, La, 35, 41, 42, 43, 64, 124, 160–163, 202, 203
Reger, Max, 50
Reicha, Antonin, 15, 16, 17, 18, 22, 26, 28, 45, 46, 48, 51, 54, 66, 124, 156, 169, 210
Reine de Saba, La (Gounod), 203
Requiem (Brahms), 163, 167
— (Cherubini), 20
— (Mozart), 46
Revue Musicale, La, 188
Reyer, Ernest, 98
Rheingold (Wagner), 69, 211
Rhené-Baton, 41
Richards, Brinley, 29
Robert le Diable (Meyerbeer), 12, 14, 69
Robin des Bois (Weber), 46
Robin Gray, 179
Roi d'Ys, Le (Lalo), 202
Roland-Manuel, 196

Rolland, Romain, 188
Romeo and Juliet (Berlioz), 64
Ropartz, J. Guy, 7, 42, 54, 81, 82, 87, 89, 180, 181, 194, 205, 207, 214
Roses et Papillons, 180
Rossini, Gioacchino, 12, 13, 21, 199
de Rothschild, Baron James, 21
Rougier, J., 122
Rousseau, Samuel, 176
Roussel, Albert, 44, 53, 57, 196, 203, 204, 207, 212
Royal Academy of Music, London, 12
— College of Music, London, 209
Royer, Alphonse, 27
Ruins of Athens (Beethoven), 46
Ruth, 23, 24, 32, 38, 40, 157–158

S

de Sainbris, Guiollot, 171
Saint-Saëns, Camille, 11, 32, 36, 37, 38, 40, 41, 47, 52, 64, 69, 71, 73, 79, 80, 95, 96, 120, 121, 133, 148, 165, 190, 193, 196, 197, 200, 201, 204, 214
Samson (Handel), 46
— *et Dalila* (Saint-Saëns), 52, 200
Satie, Erik, 196, 203, 204, 212
Schlesinger, 123
Schola Cantorum, 38, 43, 53, 73, 171, 187, 189, 193, 197, 203, 212
Scholes, Dr Percy, 69, 95
Schönberg, Arnold, 203
Schubert, Franz, 40, 52, 84, 127, 141, 211
Schuberth, 23, 123
Schumann, Robert, 12, 72, 73, 124, 126, 129, 130, 138
Scott, Sir Walter, 29
Scriabine, Alexander, 80, 94
Selva, Blanche, 196
Sermon on the Mount, 24, 25, 164, 210
de Serres, Louis, 197
de Séverac, Déodat, 196
Shepherds of the Delectable Mountains (Vaughan Williams), 166
Sibelius, Jean, 11
Siegfried (Wagner), 98
' Les Six ', 11, 176, 203, 204
Smyth, Dame Ethel, 124, 192, 193
Société des Concerts du Conservatoire, 39, 45
— Nationale de Musique, 32, 35, 37, 38, 40 190
Soleil, Le, 42, 181
Sonata (Liszt), 54
Song of Solomon, 93
Souvenance, 178
Spohr, Louis, 162

Spontini, Luigi, 12, 25, 46, 199
Stabat Mater (Pergolesi), 46
Stamboul (de Bréville), 194
Stanford, Sir Charles Villiers, 86
Storm (Lemmens), 95
Stradella, 172
Strauss, Richard, 58
Stravinsky, Igor, 176
String Quartet, 40, 42, 52
Suite-Sonata (Vitali), 56
Survey of Contemporary Music (Gray), 171
Sylphe, Le, 179
Sylvia (Delibes), 198
Symphonies (Beethoven), 20, 46, 55, 56, 84, 96
— (Brahms), 58, 84, 86, 88
Symphonie avec orgue (Saint-Saëns), 79
— cévenole (d'Indy), 79
— espagnole (Lalo), 201
— fantastique (Berlioz), 11
— première, à Grand Orchestre, 15
Symphony in G minor (Lalo), 79, 98, 201
— — — (Mozart), 84
— — — (Roussel), 53, 57
— in C major (Schubert), 84
— Fifth (Vaughan Williams), 209
— First British (Crotch), 12

T

Tallis, Thomas, 29, 30
Tannhauser (Wagner), 176
Tausig, Karl, 145, 149
Tchaikovsky, Peter, 72, 176
Temple Church, 29, 30
de Ternant, Andrew, 29, 30
Thaïs (Massenet), 200
Thamar (Balakirev), 64
Théâtre Française, 26
Theuriet, A., 181
Thibaud, Jacques, 41
Thomas, Ambroise, 21, 33, 39, 40, 47, 48, 173, 198, 199, 209
Tiersot, Jean, 179
— Julien, 54, 61
Torchet, Julien, 38
Tour de Babel, 31, 158–160, 162
Tournemire, Charles, 42, 43
Trio, A Grand, 14
— Fourth, 35, 128,
— de Salon, 127
Tristan und Isolde (Wagner), 52, 65, 66, 110
Triumphal Ode (Holmès), 179
Trois Exiles, Les, 179

U

Université, L' (Cochin), 52
Urban, Chrétien, 21

V

Vaies, Gustave, 27
Valéry, Paul, 207
Valet de Ferme, 27, 173
Vallas, Léon, 89, 98, 186, 188, 189, 199, 202, 208
Vallins, Gaston, 193
Variations on a Nursery Song (Dohnányi), 79
— Brillantes sur l'air du Pré aux Clercs, 14, 61, 143, 144
— sur la Ronde favorite de Gustave III, 14, 61
— sur un original Thème 61
— symphoniques, 38, 39, 41, 42, 50, 59, 71–79, 114, 144 ; (Boëllmann), 79
Vase Brise, Le, 180
Vaughan Williams, Ralph, 166, 209, 213
Verdi, Guiseppe, 198, 199
Véstale, La (Spontini), 12
Viardot, Mme Pauline, 178
Victoria, Queen, 23, 181, 199
Vidal, Paul, 41
Vierne, Louis, 120, 194
Village Romeo and Juliet, 94
Violin Concerto (Mendelssohn), 46
— Sonata, 38, 42, 50, 52, 57, 129, 133–138, 177
— — (d'Indy), 188
— — (Lekeu), 191
Vitali, Giovanni Battista, 56

W

Wagner, Richard, 26, 46, 80, 110, 175, 187, 192, 197, 199, 200, 202, 211, 214
Walküre, Die (Wagner), 80
War, Franco-Prussian, 31, 187, 190
Weber, Carl Maria von, 13, 46
Webern, Anton von, 203
Wesley, Samuel Sebastian, 29
Westminster Abbey, 29
Widor, Charles Marie, 96, 120, 194
Witches' Sabbath (Berlioz), 69
Wood, Sir Henry, 64, 192

Y

Ysayë, Eugene, 40, 134, 191

Z

Zimmerman, Pierre Joseph, 16, 18

THIS book is set in 11-pt Baskerville one point leaded, a type designed by the calligrapher and printer to the University of Cambridge, John Baskerville (1706-1775) of Birmingham. Baskerville is a classical type-face described as a letter embodying the most precise geometrical proportions with the greatest elegance. Its sharp precision of outline, best seen on a smooth surface paper under ideal conditions of machining, makes it the forerunner of what is now known as the series of 'moderns'.

The present design, based on the original version of about 1761, was recut in 1924 by the Monotype Corporation from whose matrices it has been cast.